Framework | **Staff Development**

Improving Boys' Performance

Geoff Hannan

Heinemann *Supporting your Professional Development*

For Richard and Andrew Peters and Harry Hamilton
(not forgetting Darren)

Editor: Karen Westall
Illustrations: Eric Jones

© 1999 Geoff Hannan

British Library Cataloguing in Publication Data. A catalogue record for this book is available from the British Library.

First published 1999
04 03 02 01
10 9 8 7 6 5 4 3 2
Heinemann Educational Publishing, Halley Court, Jordan Hill, Oxford OX2 8EJ

ISBN 0 435 04626–8 (book)
ISBN 0 435 01620–2 (book + INSET module)

Printed in the United Kingdom by Ashford Colour Press.

Contents

continued

Contents continued

Introduction

There are twice as many boys with learning difficulties as there are girls. In special units, boys outnumber girls by six to one. By seven years of age, one-third of boys compared with only one-fifth of girls are struggling to read. Five times as many boys are excluded from school. Girls outperform boys in all GCSE subjects and, generally, at A-level. Women outnumber men at university. And so it goes on. You have probably heard the statistics and, indeed, see them in action in your classroom. The gender gap in performance is getting wider and showing itself at an increasingly younger age. (Reference: SHA, *Can Boys Do Better?*, please see *Further reading*.)

Solutions and strategies

This book is designed to provide some practical learning and behaviour management solutions. It presents down-to-earth strategies for the teacher to use for improving the performance of boys. I don't have all the answers, but I know from the feedback from my INSET programmes that teachers find the strategies effective in narrowing the gender gap. They work, try them!

Pupil feedback from the Doncaster LEA Improving Performance Project where Geoff Hannan trained teachers and children in the strategies from this book.

This symbol indicates that the text in this book links to an activity in the accompanying photocopiable INSET module (available from Heinemann, ISBN 0 435 01621–0).

Darren grows up to be tough
Darren grows up to be cool
Darren grows up as the doer
But he doesn't do well at school.

Cindy grows up to be quiet
Cindy grows up to be shy
But Cindy grows up to listen
And Cindy grows up to try.

Oh Darren, don't show yourself clever
Oh Darren, don't show yourself bright
Your mates prefer you stupid
Your mates prefer you fight!

So Cindy grows up to the levels
Cindy grows up with the skills
As Darren grows up with the bruises
And society up with his ills.

From *The Secrets of Success* by Geoff Hannan

Chapter

Gender differences

Stereotyping vs. valuing differences

Stereotyping is the blanket prescription of common traits to an entire group of people. Whilst categorisation is important to our understanding of the world and of one another, stereotyping reduces uniqueness to its lowest common denominator. There are far many more differences *within* groups of people than there are *between* groups.

Good Equal Opportunities practice, on the other hand, is about valuing difference. It is about seeking to satisfy the differing needs that individuals and groups of individuals are *likely* to share because of their gender, ethnicity, social circumstance, abilities or disabilities. If we wish truly to value difference and seek to overcome the potential disadvantages that groups are likely to suffer, then we need to acknowledge these likely differences.

In what follows, I provide a profile of the average boy compared to the average girl. The profiles are designed as tools to 'fine-tune' thinking to the needs of an individual pupil. I am not saying that ALL girls are like this and ALL boys are like that. I *am* saying that boys are likely to differ from girls in the following ways and for the following reasons. The categorisations may then become practical tools that we may use as starting points to diagnose the needs of an individual child irrespective of his or her gender.

Doers and thinkers The average boy is a 'doer' first and a thinker, hopefully, second! The average girl is a thinker first and a doer, hopefully, second. In the broadest of terms, good Equal Opportunities practice in the classroom is about getting the girls into the doing and the boys into the thinking!

The typical boy has a much shorter concentration span than the typical girl. He is much more easily bored and more likely to be disruptive when he is bored. His verbal and literacy skills are weaker than hers; so, too, are his social skills and collaborative competencies. His listening skills are poor compared to hers. He is less able to think reflectively, to plan and organise his work and follow linear processes from start through to end with adequate attention to detail. She, however, tends to be overly cautious and delivers too much detail.

He is differently and highly influenced by his peer group. He is likely to overestimate his ability, she to underestimate it. She works harder and does more homework. She balances her school work with her social life: with him it's either one or the other. She is multitasked and can handle many operations simultaneously, he has to do one thing at a time. However, her confidence is lower and she is risk-averse in her behaviour.

Other differences

Whilst she can defer gratification, he seeks short-term, immediate reward and attention.

Her interest spectrum is centred upon relationships and people, his upon objects, systems and facts. He is a speculative thinker and a trial-and-error, experiential learner. She is a reflective thinker and a step-by-step, sequential learner.

Whilst the girl is in many ways a natural pupil, he is a boy first and the pupil, frequently, a poor second. She brings the chalk to the classroom, he brings the cheese!

I remind the reader that I am not seeking to present a stereotype, merely to present a list of potential learning disadvantages. No individual girl or boy will totally fit the above profiles (although some come close!). They are the bare bones of understandings on which I put the meat of this book's strategies.

But enough now of the food analogies and into a brief synopsis of probable reasons behind boys' underattainment! On to the information that every teacher, every parent, every colleague and every partner really ought to know about probable gender differences, if for no other nor finer reason than it might just help us to be a little more tolerant of one another …

Nature *and* nurture

We are what we are because of a complex interaction between 'hard-wired' genetic influences and environmental factors. Let's not get into the chicken and egg debate here. Suffice it to say that what came first is rather irrelevant to the chicken!

Brain development

There is now an accepted understanding that the brains of women and men differ to a considerable degree. All human foetuses begin in the womb as female. Six weeks or so into pregnancy, if the baby is to be a boy, testosterone bathes the womb and the foetus begins its 'struggle to be male'. As part of this process, it seems, male brains begin to develop differently. Women have language centres on both sides of their brain whereas in men they predominate in the left hemisphere. Men have more specialised visuo-spatial centres. The corpus callosum which links the right and left hemispheres of the brain is larger in women than in men (with the probable exception of some gay men and some lesbian women). Emotional centres being largely situated on the right side and language centres on the left, the woman, it seems, is quite literally more in contact with her feelings.

Child development

On average, boys are born smaller and develop language more slowly than girls. With more focused eye contact, at six weeks the girl will respond to a human face with a smile. The boy will respond whether it's a human face or a balloon! At six years, put two girls who are strangers to one another in a room with some toys and, by the end of half an hour, they will know all about one another and will be playing together. Two boys won't even know one another's names and will be playing separately. That's if they haven't had a fight in the meantime! (Please refer to *Why Men Don't Iron* – see *Further reading*.)

Let's give nature some credit in gender difference. Boys and girls are undoubtedly born with some differing genetic propensities. Propensities, however, are not destinies. Although, as a man, something in the genes helps to make me what I am, I am a few million years up the evolutionary scale from my tree-swinging, nose-breathing forebears (despite my tendency to revert to type when my football team scores a goal or anyone remotely female crosses my field of vision!). I might be an emotional dyslexic but I can learn to potty-train my animal instincts. Naked ape that I am, I am also a thinking one. Nurture, too, has its part to play.

The dolly and the toy car

Types of play

Consider the differences in learning skills development as girls and boys come out to play. Typically the girl plays with her doll and the boy with his toy car. The girl is talking to her dolly. The boy is just making noises. Her early play activity is centred on relationships with people and his on relationships with objects. He may have a rich imaginative landscape in his mind as he dashes around doing things but, unlike her, he doesn't verbalise it. Not only does her play enrich and develop her language skills but also, early on, she begins to sequence her activities and follow linear processes. She will make up stories. Her stories will have a clear beginning, a progression and an end. He starts playing at or with something, stops and plays with something else.

Now consider how much in learning is sequential, how much is about following linear progressions and how much is about seeing things through from start to end.

Girls' skills

Consider, too, the traditional stereotypical influences that affect the girl. She is more likely to help with the housework, go shopping and look after younger brothers and sisters. She is learning to take responsibility for herself and others in extended time frames. She is entrusted with tasks that develop her maturity. She learns to be attentive, neat and cautious. With some genetic propensities in this direction, she learns to be caring and responsible. By Year 1 (P2), she has already developed many learning advantages over her male classmate. She can even sit at a desk without fidgeting!

Boys' skills

This is not to say that the average boy isn't developing skills in other areas. He certainly is. He's a great explorer, more inclined to venture into new domains and seek wild and new experiences. On his trusty steed, with mighty sword in hand, he sallies forth to extend the reaches of his confidence; heroically and single-handedly to slay the dragons of fear and injustice.

Playtime finishes with girls and boys sharing many similarities but also with some differences. In terms of learning skills, the boys come in with more bruises!

Advice to parents

A word to the parents amongst you. To develop your small son's language skills, it is likely to be of little use giving him a doll to play with. It is little use adapting girls' toys for boys. It is not '"My Little Pony" goes to the abattoir'! To develop his language skills, sit down with him as he plays with his car and get him to make up stories about it. Get him to verbalise more. And dads … you be the one who reads to him! You are an important role model to your young son. Don't let him grow up to think that it is just the women who read and talk about feelings.

Many parents will buy their daughters constructional toys and then discover that they prefer playing with their dolls. Indeed, a girl is only likely to play with building bricks if she can make a little house with it, put a little person in the house and then make up a story. So sit down with her and get her to experiment more and take more risks in her play. Rough and tumble play is good for her too as it helps to develop her confidence. Mums … do non-stereotypical things with your daughters!

Dinner party man

Progression in communication

Listen to people talking in, say, a pub or a restaurant and you will hear a sequence of communication emerge. The conversation will progress through the stages of Descriptive–Reflective–Speculative in that order!

Indeed, if you study any scenario where people are communicating well with others you are likely to find this progression. From simple sentence exchanges between neighbours in the street, to complex interactions like a dinner party, this hierarchy is there.

Consider 'Nice day, isn't it?' 'Better than yesterday!' 'I wonder if it will last?'... even here, the sequence is Descriptive–Reflective–Speculative!

Now observe a typical dinner party. Conversations are heavily descriptive to begin with. People describe how they got there! They then proceed to describe recent activities in the past, for example, the holiday they have just been on. This takes the form, at first, of a blow-by-blow account of what they *did* on holiday: it's descriptive. Then it becomes reflective as feelings are attached to the actions previously described. People now go on to discuss what they liked or disliked about the holiday. Finally, when everyone is relaxed or drunk or both the conversation becomes speculative. Deep philosophical conversations occur always at the end of the dinner party! Now study other communication systems a little more deeply and you will find that the Descriptive–Reflective–Speculative hierarchy is prevalent everywhere.

In counselling, step one is to describe your feelings. Step two is to reflect upon the feelings previously described. Step three is to be speculative: how can you make yourself feel better? In the Management of Change, step one is to be descriptive, so you audit. Step two is to be reflective so from the audit you analyse an organisation's strengths and weaknesses. Step three is to be speculative: how do you build upon the strengths to overcome the weaknesses?

The hierarchy in lessons

A good lesson will follow this hierarchy. When things go wrong in the classroom, it is frequently because these steps are missing or out of sequence.

In a lesson on drugs education the teacher's starting point was 'what can we do about the problems of drugs?' Her start was speculative, communication was strained and the children's behaviour quickly deteriorated.

This lesson should have been as follows. Stage One (Descriptive): *'You have five minutes. With the person next to you, write down ten things you would think of as being drugs.'* Stage Two (Reflective): *'Draw a line down your page. Select one of your drugs and see if you can find five good things and five bad things about it.'* Stage Three (Speculative): *'Now select one of your bad things and let's discuss what we might do about it!'*

Descriptive–Reflective–Speculative is how we communicate. It is also how we think and learn!

Communicating differently

However, men and women use the hierarchy differently!

From simple to complex interactions, gender differences in this hierarchy are easy to hear.

Woman: *Nice day, isn't it? Better than yesterday!* (Descriptive–Reflective)
Man: *Nice day, isn't it? I wonder if it will last?* (Descriptive–Speculative)

Now revisit the dinner party and note the gender differences. We find that, when the conversation is descriptive, men and women are contributing equally to the discussion. Midway through the dinner party as the conversation becomes reflective, the women are doing most of the talking. Finally, when it gets heavy and deep at the end of the party, the men take over, and the women might well be sitting back embarrassed by their partners!

The dinner party illustrates many gender traits. The man is a speculative thinker and communicator. He presents an argument and then post justifies it. He polarises. Something is either right or wrong. And he, of course, has to be right! He is confrontational: 'I am right and you are wrong!' The woman is largely a reflective thinker and communicator. She communicates and thinks in the grey holistic area between the extremes of right and wrong. He has the mindset 'I think' and speaks largely to communicate information and fact. She has the mindset 'I feel' and speaks to communicate her feelings. Her approach is conciliatory rather than confrontational and she is much more likely to explore the whole issue. Finally, her ease at communication itself allows her to think whilst talking. He works out what he is going to say and then says it! Men and women communicate differently. Men and women *think* differently.

DIY man

Differing gender approaches

You can obtain major insights into boys' underattainment through a little observation of their adult counterparts. Their poor reflective skills present a major weakness in their learning; their inadequate process skills perhaps an even bigger one! Consider self-assembly furniture and the differing gender approaches to it.

Most women will go to the instructions first and follow them step by step. Most men go straight to the wood and start to assemble it. He *does* first whilst she organises, plans and *thinks* first. Let's develop the scenario a little further …

He gets to do the job. After all, it's homemaking, it's our hunter-gatherer propensity, it's working with objects and he's expected to be good at it! He is a speculative thinker too, whose male identity is rooted in his ability to solve problems. Why read the instructions? Any problems that emerge he'll be able to deal with as they occur, no sweat! But, of course, as a man, he overestimates his ability! He soon discovers that his skill levels do not support his confidence. Reluctantly he picks up the instructions. Luckily they are in the form of diagrams. Let's face it: he wouldn't bother to read them if they were in words. But now he is beginning to get frustrated and reverts to the level of a five-year-old child. At five, when a child bumps into something, it is always the something's fault. 'Naughty chair!' the five-year-old cries. 'Bloody wood!' yells DIY man. No, no, it's not his skill level that is bad, it's the object he's working with!

Now, men are either brilliant or awful but seldom mediocre, whilst you women frequently luxuriate in mediocrity! You could be brilliant but your rotten risk-taking skills and low confidence stop you. Like a girl at school, you do too much work: you go over and over the same things to make yourself feel totally secure and safe before you cautiously move on. Like a little boy at school, DIY man now goes one of two ways.

Giving up or completing the task

Ineffectual DIY man or boy at school gives up. He will now get easily diverted away from the task in hand to something more immediately gratifying. They say that this is why men collect things far more than women do! He has a row with his woman. Unable to deal with the emotional difficulties of the moment, he picks up a newspaper and weeps in a general way for mankind instead! Or he goes to his den and fiddles with his stamp collection. Thus bad DIY man gives up and like a Year 11 (S5) boy with his course work, will need to be nagged back into doing it.

At his best, however, DIY man, when faced with a problem, will stay with it until it's solved. Take the computer as an example here. This highlights his experiential learning strengths. A new computer program is learnt experientially. You download and play with it. The woman's linear learning style means that she prefers to follow a manual step by step. Here, she is the one at a disadvantage for these days there is no manual. If he has a problem with his new program, he'll be up all night to solve it. If she finds difficulty, she'll stop and get someone to tell her how to do it.

Either way, and eventually, DIY man completes the task. Now remember the boy's need for immediate gratification? The first thing DIY man will now do is to call his partner in and show her the furniture. And, please note, now she dare not criticise!

When dinner party woman meets DIY man

Solving problems

It would be remiss of me, at this point, not to mention how these simple observations are useful to us all.

When a woman has a problem, she wants her partner to sit down and listen to her talk through this problem. Talking through the problem helps her to solve her problem herself. She does not want or need, yet frequently gets, DIY man. Rather than simply and actively listening to her, he is likely to sit there making suggestions. For all the best reasons, he is doing the wrong thing. She then turns to him and says 'You don't listen to me!' And she is absolutely correct. If you have a female colleague or partner, then, men, you need to give her time to let her talk through things. Ask questions, don't try to problem-solve for her! Similarly, if you have an adolescent daughter, don't tell her what to do! This builds barriers between daughters and parents (especially mothers!). Give her time to talk through her own ideas and problems.

DIY man is a solitary problem-solver. When he's got a problem, he wants to go away and crack it on his own. He does not talk through his feelings, he works them out himself or disperses them through doing things. Dinner party woman feels rejected on these occasions that he doesn't need her support. Women, give him space! He is just different, that's all it is!

If you have an adolescent son avoid nagging him! You know it doesn't do the slightest bit of good. Give him the knowledge that you are always available if he does wish to talk things through. Try to be non-judgemental. To get him to talk to you, *do* something with him. He is more likely to open up at half-time watching a football match.

Put nature/nurture and your sons and your daughters together with DIY and Dinner party man and what do you get? Subject outcomes at school!

Learning styles and subject outcomes

More boy-friendly subjects	Girl-friendly subjects
Maths	English
Physics	Modern Languages
Physical Education	Religious Education
	PSE
	Music
	Art
	Drama
	Integrated Humanities
	Biology
	Chemistry
	(History)
	(Geography)
	(Technology)
Objects and/or systems based	**People based**
Speculative	**Reflective**
Experiential learning	**Linear learning**
Doing based	**Language based**

The National Curriculum

The prime understanding for the provision and delivery of Equal Opportunities is that BOYS AND GIRLS HAVE DIFFERING LEARNING STYLES.

Rightly or wrongly, the English National Curriculum is much more girl-friendly than boy-friendly. This 'feminisation' is easy to see in the changed outcome patterns in subjects such as technology, geography and history (in brackets, above, for this reason). Technology is boy-friendly when it is about doing and making things. The pre- and post-realisation emphasis of the National Curriculum places it now firmly in the girl-friendly reflective and analytical arena. Boys hold on well to factual information and like working with it. A history curriculum that is centred in fact is boy-friendly, whereas one based on evidence seeking and analysis is girl-friendly.

Only in maths and physics is the gap a small one. These are black and white subjects. You are either right or wrong. There is no grey area in which the girls can thrive. With their strong learning skills and hard work, they do well in the midrange of results but don't achieve the higher grades as frequently as the boys. It is important to note, however, that the best girl in maths is always comparable to the best boy and vice versa in English. There are just not as many of them up there at the top.

Don't despair

Whether or not you agree in part or in whole with my theory of gender differences, there are things you can do in the classroom to improve the performance of boys. You will find that the strategies in this book, whilst developed from the understandings above, are not dependent upon them. They are good educational strategies irrespective of gender. However, they improve the performance of boys more than they improve the performance of girls. We should be seeking to diminish the gender gap not obliterate it. Given the above, girls should do better than the boys. Where schools have no gender gap or where the boys are outperforming the girls, we must challenge their practice. Girls, and especially working-class girls, are still underperforming in many areas. The strategies in this book will improve the performance of girls as well as boys, but not by as much. Thus they endeavour to narrow the gap and not to close it.

Chapter
2

Go for five

The teaching of linear process skills

Bet a boy that he can't do something and he'll pretty soon prove you wrong! Learning is an intellectually active process. Communicate challenge more and it will help to motivate boys into activity.

Setting challenges

Variety is a highly important key for all children in their learning, boys especially so. Think 'challenge' and with a small step of the imagination you can turn even the potentially dullest of curriculum areas into an adventure! Studying a book could become a five-day detective game played in teams. Early foreign language learning could become a space journey to an alien planet where the brave astronauts are preparing themselves for mankind's first contact. The Key Stage 3 science class could become a laboratory team seeking a new industrial process for using magnets. Maths can become code-breaking.

Communicating challenge at the start of a more traditional lesson will help to motivate the pupils. Tell the class that they are going to find today's lesson difficult … they'll be able to do it … but they are going to find it hard! And you are helping immediately to make it more 'boy friendly'. Be a little sensitive to the girls' reaction, however. Bet a girl she can't do it and she might well agree with you! Here is your opportunity to talk about the way that girls tend to underestimate themselves and boys overestimate their skill levels. Use it.

Time sequences

Another important ingredient especially, although not exclusively, for boys is 'time'. A good rule of thumb is to go for short time sequences rather than long ones. It is better for boys to work intensively for short periods of time rather than half-heartedly for longer periods during which they have plenty of opportunity for distraction or creeping lethargy. Break extended work down into manageable smaller units.

As part of your variety of process, sequentially extend times on task. Rather than teaching for half an hour and then the pupils working for half an hour, it is frequently better to teach part one for five minutes – pupils work part one for five minutes: teach part two for ten minutes – pupils work part two for ten minutes and so on. Make activities at the start of the lesson 'quick-fire' ones designed to engage and motivate and, as the lesson proceeds, progressively lengthen the time the pupils are working – thus extending their concentration by stages.

Homework

Always apply a time structure to your homework assignments. Boys will be more likely to do them! Girls do their duty first and then have their fun. With boys, it is reversed. Girls are much more likely to do their homework first thing in the evening. The boy goes to his computer game first and by the time he's finished there's no time or incentive for his homework! The more open-ended the homework in terms of how long it might take, the less likely he is to do it. If you say that a particular piece of homework will take the class thirty minutes and at the end of thirty minutes they can stop if they wish to, boys are more likely to do it first. Boys tend to put things on the back burner if they think they might take a long time.

Communicate the purpose

I wrote earlier about the male need for immediate gratification. This makes the communication of *purpose* especially important to boys. 'Why am I doing this? What's in this lesson for me?' These are questions you should answer by clearly communicating the purpose of your classroom and homework activities.

Communicate relevance in 'Pupil Speak' at the start of the lesson: 'during today's lesson you will be learning this, this and this.' Tell the class why it is relevant. Not because the curriculum demands it but how relevant it is to themselves and their learning! At the end of the lesson, check and get the class to check that they have actually learnt this something. Use more quizzes. These are particularly useful in aiding the younger boys' motivation. 'Learn this for homework and tomorrow first thing we are going to have a quiz.' Not a test. Test is teacher versus pupil: quiz is pupil versus pupil and picks up on boys' competitive nature. Have extra merit points or even small prizes for those who do well and have put in a lot of effort.

Quality not quantity

And one final point before we get on to a more specific strategy: go for quality not quantity. One sentence or paragraph well written with time and care taken over it is better in learning than several pages reluctantly scrawled. Remember that we learn nothing *by* writing. (More, lots more, about that later!) But first: try this …

Go for five and use five steps

This very simple and easily applied strategy helps pupils to sequence and structure their ideas and their learning. It works like this:

Five solutions

Let's say that you have a problem to solve. *First think of five possible solutions to the problem and then select one.*

You now get a far stronger solution to your problem. Using the 'male' speculative strength, followed by the 'female' skill of reflective analysis, allows you to get quickly and deeply into possibilities and find an appropriate course of action. You may find that you can only think of three solutions. But if you 'go for five', you are more likely to have found the third!

**Five steps
to an action**

Now find five steps in taking the selected action. You are now breaking the process down into manageable stages. If you use this procedure for action planning, then you will be much more likely to achieve your goal. The enactment will have enough precision without being over complicated and too unwieldy to handle. Go back to the profiles of the typical boy and the typical girl and you might see straight away how useful it is. The boy is likely to underprepare, finding just three steps. The girl is inclined to be over elaborate and develops seven or so steps! It extends the boy's planning and appropriately clarifies the girl's.

GOING FOR FIVE can be applied across the curriculum! Take written work, for example.

History

A history class is writing an essay: 'What were the effects of poverty on Victorian England?' Instruct them not to write anything yet. Tell them first to *find five possible effects that poverty might have had, such as poor health and crime.* Before beginning their essay, ask them to make five single word notes at the top of the page. Next, instruct the class to write a paragraph for each of their ideas in turn: a paragraph that goes Descriptive–Reflective, that is, states each individual idea and explains it. You are now providing a scaffold for the pupils to order, sequence and express their ideas. Again, this strategy turns out to be especially (although not exclusively) useful for the boys. Key Stage 4 pupils especially will find this approach useful as an examination strategy.

Science

Now consider a science class that has just completed an experiment.
Before writing up your experiment, look for five steps in what you have just done. The class is now reviewing the experiment with enough (and not too much) detail to remember it and to learn from it.

Food technology

In food technology …
'Before I begin the demonstration, put the numbers one to five down the page in your exercise book, leaving two lines between each.'
Deliver the demonstration in five steps and, at the end of each, instruct the pupils to write a few words to remind them of what to do.
'Boys make sure to write enough so that you will remember what to do and in what order! Girls don't write too much … trust yourself to remember what to do!'
You will see how the boys now engage in the activity more carefully and sequentially and how they remember the process better. And you will notice, too, how the girls get down more quickly to the making rather than just the organisation.

Drama

The drama lesson …
'You have five full minutes' planning time. Sit down with your group and plan five things that are going to happen in your playlet. OK boys … one thing can be a slow-motion fight!! But you have got to show me <u>three</u> things that lead up to it and, after it, one consequence!'
This is a particularly useful way of getting a more planned and thoughtful approach in boys' drama.

English

In English …
'Let's see if we can find <u>five</u> words that describe the character of Macbeth.'
'I am going to show you <u>five</u> things to look for in analysing a poem.'

Modern languages

In modern languages …
'Schreiben Sie, bitte, <u>fünf</u> Wörter für …' (Write five words please for …)

Geography

In geography …
'As your partner reads the paragraph on Switzerland, make notes under the following <u>five</u> headings: Terrain, Climate, People, Imports and Exports. You will then tell us what you have discovered about the country.'

Music

In music …
'As you listen to the music, I want you to try to find <u>five</u> words that might describe it. You will then be asked to explain why you chose the words you did.'

Maths

In maths, you will find that trying to find five steps to a mathematical operation, or in science, five steps to an experiment, will help pupils sequence and remember the process better.

Why five?

Listen out for this magic number! There is something deeply significant about five in our thinking. We are advised to take more exercise. How often? <u>Five</u> half-hour sessions a week. We are advised to eat more fruit and vegetables. How much? You guessed it! <u>Five</u> portions of fruit or vegetables per day!

How many styles of writing are there in National Curriculum English? Well, <u>five</u>, of course! The government puts forward a new plan. How many points to it? More often than not it will be a <u>five-point</u> plan.

**Five is
ubiquitous**

From the five working days in the week to the Five Pillars of Islam, this number, more than any other, has significance to us. Our decimal system is based on the abacus system of five. It will be because we have five digits on the hand. It will be because that's how we learn to count and to order things when small. It will be because, it seems, our brains hold onto things best in odd rather than even numbers. Quite unconsciously, you will break down information you want to recall into groups of threes and fives, rather than twos or fours, or sixes. Try to recall an eight-digit number and you are likely to end up forgetting one of the digits because the circuitry of our brains is wired into odd rather than even 'bites'. Seven seems to be the maximum in short-term recall, five is optimum.

Whatever the reasons behind it, five is ubiquitous. A five-paragraphed history essay is a strong essay and scores high marks. Just as a three-point political plan is rather bland and a seven-point plan unmemorable, why five? Because four is too few and six is too many.

Try this in the classroom and note the different responses from the boys and the girls. Use this activity to illustrate how finding five ideas helps to develop our thinking and five steps helps to develop our planning. As well as using GOING FOR FIVE, get the pupils to understand WHY they should go for five.

The desert island and the mirror

Tell the class that they are about to be stranded on a desert island. Fortunately, they are prepared for such everyday eventualities. They have a survival kit. In this survival kit is a mirror.

Five steps

Step One: Challenge them to find five separate uses that a mirror might have to help their survival.

Step Two: Select one of the uses, for example: to signal to a passing ship.

Step Three: Challenge them to find five important steps in using the mirror to signal for help. There are five significant ones:
1. Go to high ground.
2. Flash the mirror.
3. Look for a response.
4. Use Morse Code to relay a message for help.
5. Look again for a response that gives you instructions.
Notice how the boys are likely to miss out steps whilst the girls are too elaborate. Notice how the girls want to clean the mirror first! Notice, however, how much more thought they give to the situation compared to the boys. The typical man stands on the beach and flashes the mirror with no chance of it being seen and the typical woman works out elaborate plans for using the mirror, by which time the ship has gone!

Step Four: Challenge the class to select a different use of the mirror and work out the five steps themselves.

Step Five: Discuss how useful GOING FOR FIVE is and when they might use it to help their planning and analysis.

Look no hands

There is too much reliance on hands going up in the classroom. When a teacher asks for hands to go up, it is only the more confident pupils who are involved. It is also bad gender practice for girls. The ratio of boys to girls putting hands up in the classroom is on average three to one in favour of the boys. Try counting next time!

Added to this, many pupils, like adults, require thinking space prior to answering questions. Give them this space and you then build their confidence and develop their reflective skills. Try this, especially at the start of the lesson …

*'Here is my question … talk with the person next to you … you have just two minutes to find me **five** answers to my question.'*

After the two minutes, still don't allow hands to go up. Instead, choose as many pupils as you can to participate and take responses from them *quickly* using affirmation and praise …
Affirmation (repeating back the pupil's response): *'Using a melon!'*
Praise: *'A good idea!'*

Participation

You are now doing some important things! You are requiring all the pupils actively to participate right then and there at the start of the lesson. Their involvement is now far more likely to be sustained. You are requiring the class to be reflective, to think before doing. You are structuring on-task talk at the start of the lesson. This is an important strategy. Structure on-task talk and you get less off-task talk! A simple mental check-list as you take responses can now ensure that girls and boys answer questions equally. The boys still get three times the attention in the average classroom. (If you don't believe this then get someone to count during your lessons.)

In using TALK WITH THE PERSON NEXT TO YOU, you are requiring the girls to take risks in presenting their opinions and ideas whilst allowing an opportunity for less confident boys as well as girls to prepare their responses. You are affording opportunities for immediate verbal praise (thus gratification) which is especially useful to the motivation of boys. You are also giving yourself opportunities quietly to get children on-task as you wander around the class.

And importantly, this strategy allows you to start the lesson with the pupils' own understandings and gives you an opportunity to assess those understandings. Use this strategy at the start of your lessons periodically and the pace will be livened. TALK WITH THE PERSON NEXT TO YOU is a simple idea that values the pupil's view as the fundamental starting point for learning. Try it!

In Key Stage 4 especially, *talk with the person next to you and find five* is a useful strategy for revising the content of a previous lesson before moving on.

And finally

Ending the lesson

At the end of the lesson …

'Talk with the person next to you and devise a really difficult question to ask me about what you have just learnt. See if we can get five good questions from the class!'

Don't allow hands to go up. Go round the class again. Now you are requiring pupils to review and evaluate their own understandings and to define their gains in learning to themselves.

Put these strategies together and you are actively teaching pupils two fundamental learning skills: to present ideas and to ask questions.

Challenge … you have five minutes … to improve the quality of boys' learning, can you think of five other ways you might use the above strategies?!

The new approach

- Demanding all the pupils actively to participate.
- Actively requiring them to be reflective and to use the thinking skill of GOING FOR FIVE.
- Structuring on-task talk at the start so that you will get less off-task talk during the lesson.
- Giving equal attention to girls and boys by an easily managed mental check.
- Demanding girls take risks in presenting their opinions and ideas.
- Allowing less confident children an opportunity to prepare their response.
- Affording opportunities for immediate verbal praise.
- Giving yourself opportunities quietly to get children on-task by going around the class.
- Allowing you to start the lesson with the pupils' own understandings and allowing you to assess them.
- Quickening the pace of the lesson.

All in one simple strategy that values the child's view as the fundamental starting point for learning.

3 *Use templates*

Developing planning and thinking skills

Below are the 'templates' I have developed to aid the thinking, planning and organisational skills that boys in particular need to improve their learning. Although the concept is multi-adaptable, the ones below are subject specific to illustrate in detail how, and for what reasons, they may be effectively employed. They all work on the basis of structuring 'on-task talk' so I shall begin with the English template to explain the premises.

English template

Writer's note sheet

I want to show or explore ...

_____

_____

1. My story starts like this:
   The scene:
   The characters:
   Their feelings/mood:

2. Then this happens _____

   _____

3. Then this happens _____

   _____

4. Then this happens _____

   _____

5. My story ends like this:
   The scene:
   The characters:
   Their feelings/mood:

Some interesting words and phrases I am going to use ...

How it works

You give each pupil in the class a copy of the template on p.24 and, with a partner, instruct them to invent and talk through a story, say for ten minutes (prescribing time). On the template, they are to make short notes to remind themselves of what they are going to write about. After the ten minutes, they then write their individual stories and this will take them twenty minutes. You also tell them that, after writing their stories, they will be reading them to one another (prescribing purpose to the activity).

Oracy precedes literacy. If pupils talk through an activity prior to doing it then they will do it better. The template, using GOING FOR FIVE, leads them through the important story-making considerations sequentially and helps them to focus and structure their work.

In story-making, boys seldom express feelings ('Big boys don't cry!'). Good stories, however, rely on mood transition. If a character starts happy and ends sad, for example, this leads naturally to plot considerations: what happens to change things. This consideration thus requires the *reflective* analysis that boys especially need to improve their work. Simultaneously, it is helping the girl to simplify her over-elaborate analysis. During the ten-minute planning phase, the girl is also demanded to go straight for content rather than getting her tippex out!

The last box in the template is about the 'deconstructing of language' and I shall refer to this strategy in detail in Chapter 6.

All the templates are designed to be used as part of a variety of activities, not all the time so that they become boring but consistently, every few weeks or so, actively to teach process skills.

Technology template

The technology template is designed for both planning and post-analysis and on p.28 I suggest some other ways you might use *all* the templates to enrich variety in the classroom.

Technologist's process sheet

Date: _____

To: _____
_____

I will use:

I will:

Step one:
Step two:
Step three:
Step four:
Step five:

This went well:

1. _____
2. _____
3. _____

This went not so well!

_____

Why? _____

Next time I should:

How to use it

As part of a varied 'diet', *periodically* use the technology template as follows.

Prior to engaging in the technological task and after a teacher demonstration (perhaps in five sections!), the pupils are each given the template and allocated planning time to complete it …

'You have ten minutes. With your partner, talk through the process you will use and, in each box, write down just a few notes or a diagram to remind yourself of the steps you will be taking and the order you will be taking them in. Make sure that you find five steps in your planning.'

You should, of course, also debrief the *purpose* in using the template …

'This activity will help you to put enough detail into your planning to complete your design realisation successfully.'

Ensure that nobody commences the realisation until the ten minutes are up. Use the time, as you move around the classroom, to extend the thinking of the higher attainer and assist the lower attainer. The instruction 'or a diagram' should help the latter in completing the pre-realisation phase on time.

When the time is up, make sure that all pupils now get into the making phase and set an appropriate time for this activity. Ensure that the girls, too, start making the product!

Evaluation

On completion of the realisation phase give the following instruction …

'You have ten minutes to evaluate the process you have used by finding three things that you feel went especially well and writing these in the THIS WENT WELL boxes. Take care with your writing. Write your statements neatly and check the spelling of words you are not sure of. Use the correct technological terminology. I shall write some of the words you might wish to use on the board. Write in short sentences and take care over your punctuation as well.'

Explain the purpose …

'This will help you when you come to revise your work and when you answer examination questions. It is important to express your ideas accurately and concisely using the correct terms.'

'Finally, when you have done this, in the THIS WENT NOT SO WELL box evaluate one thing you found especially difficult or something you were not so happy with in the task you've been through; and, importantly, target an improvement: by stating how you would do it differently next time to improve your performance.'

Explain the purpose …

'This will help you to develop your evaluation and self-assessment skills and help to improve the way you do things next time.'

Varying the use of the templates

The templates may be used effectively and periodically on an individual basis, in pairs and in small groups using the same template.

You will also find the template system useful in helping the pupils to present their experiences to others in the class, thus further enriching core skills development work and helping to build their confidence.

Example

> *'In your working groups and now you have filled in your templates, I am going to ask you to take these sheets to another group and in turn make a report to them on how your group conducted the realisation and how you evaluated it. After you have made your report, it is 'question time'. The other group should try and find some really difficult questions to ask you. For example, you might like to ask them to explain why they did things in the order that they did them and not in another sequence. Through this activity you will be doing some important things in your learning.*
>
> - *You are helping to develop clear communication skills. This is important not just in your school work but outside school as well. Communication skills are very important to develop good teamwork practices which are used a lot today in the workplace.*
> - *You will also be justifying and defending your ideas which helps to build your confidence.*
> - *You are learning to criticise others constructively and to take constructive criticism yourself.*
> - *And finally, it will help you to remember what exactly it is that you have been learning!'*

Use templates to differentiate

One group might be given, for example, an intricate task to develop their organisational and design skills.

'Now that you have decided what you are going to make and as a group filled in the template, to really challenge you to look in detail at the realisation process, I am going to give this group five more templates! The challenge is to break each of your initial steps down into five smaller ones!'

Another group might be given a task to develop their teamwork skills.

'Now that you have completed your template, allocate responsibilities within your group so that each team member is responsible for a different step in the making. Being in charge of this step will help to develop your team leadership skills.'

A third group might be given a template to evaluate the work of other groups during the making.

'Your group will be a Quality Control Team during today's lesson. Whilst the other groups are planning, you must plan your quality control process using the five steps.'

Think about the potential of devising, say, three separate group work tasks which, put together, encompass all the learning objectives of a particular programme of study. When the groups present back and examine one another's work, they will be covering much of the curriculum in a shorter period of time! You should find the template system very effective in this.

Science template

The science template is designed to be used after an experiment to encourage dialogue and analysis. It requires the pupils to look in enough but not too much detail at their experiment and to extract a simple and significant statement of learning. This should be written neatly, using correct scientific terminology. Short sentences help pupils to remember information and short sentences in short paragraphs get good marks in science exams!

Scientist's analysis sheet

Date: _____

Experiment: _____
_____

I did:

| Step one: |
| Step two: |
| Step three: |
| Step four: |
| Step five: |

I discovered: _____
_____

I have learnt: _____
_____

Modern languages template

The modern languages template is designed as a tool for helping pupils to appreciate and use grammatical structures. A sentence is cut up into its constituent words and the task is, with a partner, to put the words in the correct order on the template. Build up a resource base of different key grammatical structures. One is done for you as an example.

French speakers cut and paste grammar game

Who:	
Doing:	
When:	
How/with/in what manner:	
Where:	

Here is an example …

JE	PARLE	À HUIT HEURES
TU	PARLES	AVEC MON CHAT
ELLE	PARLE	AVEC NOTRE CHAT
ILS	PARLENT	AVEC LEURS AMIS
NOUS	PARLONS	AVEC NOS AMIS
VOUS	PARLEZ	À L'ÉCOLE

Speculation template

For any speculative process, use the speculation template to teach the linear skill behind effective problem-solving. Try to solve the problem below without assistance and then see how useful the template system can be in helping you!

John says 'I didn't do it!'
Varindar says 'He's lying!'
Cindy says 'I am innocent!'
Two people are lying. Who did it?

Speculation sheet

I want to find out: _____

I think that: I can test this by:

Result:

I now think that: I can test this by:

Result:

I now think that: I can test this by:

Result:

I have discovered that:

Debrief (if you need it now!)

I want to find out: *Who did it (not who is lying! You can't discover this until you find who did it!)*
I think that: *Yes, you have to 'guess and test' to solve the problem.*
I can test this by: *Assume that John did it and see if it fits the facts that two are lying.*
The solution is at the bottom of the page.

Have a go with the templates and experiment: make some more up yourself. Just remember the key ingredients: structured on-task talk within a set time and, of course, GOING FOR FIVE.

Photocopiable templates are included in the INSET module.

Solution: Cindy did it!

A third, a third, a third

Developing group work

Structuring pair and group work

This is quite possibly *the* most important strategy you can apply for improving boys' performance. I recommend that, of your group work, one-third should be friendship pairings and groupings; one-third in single-gender non-friendship pairings and groupings; and one-third in mixed-gender pairings and groupings. And this should take the form of a 'rolling programme' of such group work so that during the time-span of half a term, all pupils work in a *structured* way with every other pupil in the class.

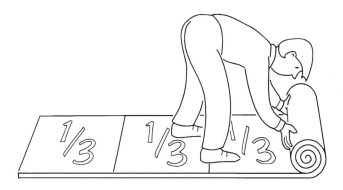

What one mostly sees in schools is informal friendship pairings in the classroom. Children who are friends with one another sit together and, although working individually, are allowed to communicate if they need to.

If you take one worksheet or book away and instruct them to work together on the task you are now into Proximal Learning and new opportunities for skills development open up …

Rationale

There are fundamentally two ways that children (and for that matter, adults as well) learn anything: individually and 'proximally', i.e. together with another child. If you listen in on two children working together on a task, you may readily appreciate the importance and the unique qualities of this type of learning. They are explaining things to one another in appropriate language and discussing new concepts at their level of comprehension. In short, they are extending their conceptual understandings and learning skills on a pupil-centred level that the adult would find difficult, if not impossible, to communicate on. Quite simply, adults express ideas differently. Consider learning something new and difficult yourself. Clearly, you would need a good teacher. But also consider the added benefits of having another new learner working with you in unravelling, say, a new and difficult concept.

Improving communication

In the school classroom, there are also many other benefits to this approach.

When two boys work together on a task, often one will take the lead and the other will follow, with little language interaction between them. Put that boy with a girl and you will find much more communication will take place. Analyse the quality of the communication and you will soon discover that the boy is now having to be REFLECTIVE and the girl SPECULATIVE, helping to compensate for likely gender disadvantage. The boy is having to defend his highly confident yet, quite probably, highly dubious speculations and reappraise them! The girl is required to be speculative: to extend beyond what to her are easy reflections into presenting and justifying alternative propositions. The upshot is that both are now enhancing and developing core language and learning skills. Simultaneously, you are helping the boy to extend his social skills.

Learning by teaching

Apply the A THIRD, A THIRD, A THIRD pluralism to this process and you are giving all pupils in the class periodic and structured access to the high-order language and learning skills of the most gifted. This is a mutually enriching access. A high-attaining pupil, in helping a low-attaining pupil, is learning to simplify, express and explain his or her understandings. Ironically, one of the ways we actually learn most effectively is through teaching! In teaching someone else, we have to structure and sequence our own understandings and express them in a form that is easily accessible. Consider the importance of this skill to examinations! Remember, however, A THIRD, A THIRD, A THIRD means that the most able are also working together to consolidate and extend their own high-level skills.

Building confidence

In applying THIRD–THIRD–THIRD, you are also developing a classroom environment that is effective in developing girls' confidence. Structured access to working with boys will help to develop especially the girls' self-assertion skills and their ability to deal with male dominance and attention-seeking.

Improving behaviour

Advantages of group work

In structuring group work in this way, you are also facilitating good behaviour in the classroom. You will find that A THIRD, A THIRD, A THIRD works in two ways for producing an easier classroom to manage.

It breaks up the blocks of potentially troublesome friendship groups of boys which give teachers most irritation. For two-thirds of the group work time they are not physically together with their friends and are required to co-operate with other pupils in the class.

Importantly, as well, you are helping all pupils in your class to feel more confident and comfortable with one another. You will find, after a while, that there will be far fewer 'put-downs' and that the pupils will be getting on much better with one another. A THIRD, A THIRD, A THIRD is a fundamental antibullying practice and for similar reasons a highly important antiracist and antisexist strategy.

Sadly, two children may be in the same class with one another for five years without once ever working together. What practical use are our antiracist policies when, for example, Asian and white pupils are never actively encouraged to work together? Neither will boys and girls work together unless we demand it. The class remains, too often, a group of strangers. You have the opportunity in your classroom to develop something far more important than learning your subject. You have the opportunity to develop tolerance and respect between the sexes and the races!

One final point. The children who most need to develop their social experience and interpersonal skills in this way are the ones least likely to be given the opportunities. Group work is perceived to be more trouble than it's worth with the more challenging 'working-class' child (and boy specifically!). One observes far more group work in schools with a 'middle-class' catchment. All children need access to these competencies. Here's how …

Managing the development

It is recommended that you begin to work in this way from scratch with a new Year 7 (S1) or with an older class that you have established a good relationship with. If you are not used to working in this way, then use the strategy with just one of your Year 7 (S1) classes for one whole term to train yourself. Then you'll be able to adopt it with your other Year 7s (S1). I strongly recommend a department policy that supports this practice.

Sit this new Year 7 (S1) class, initially, boy–girl around the room. Immediately, you will find the classroom calmer and easier to manage. Then it is important to tell the class at the outset how and why you intend to use A THIRD, A THIRD, A THIRD. A good way of doing this is to display a poster such as the one on p.36 and discuss it in detail with your class, proactively confronting their reservations. After all, their reluctance only comes from their embarrassment.

Department policy

OUR WAYS OF WORKING

DURING LESSONS YOU WILL BE WORKING IN THE FOLLOWING WAYS
FOR THE FOLLOWING REASONS:

1. **INDIVIDUALLY**
   To develop your own individual learning skills
   and enjoyment of our subject.

2. IN **FRIENDSHIP** PAIRINGS AND GROUPINGS
   To learn to help one another and work co-operatively.
   To develop your communication skills.
   To learn 'experientially' – to learn through doing things yourself
   <u>and</u> with others.

3. IN **NON-FRIENDSHIP** PAIRINGS AND GROUPINGS
   Some of the time in mixed-gender groupings.
   Some of the time in mixed-race groupings.
   To learn about and co-operate with people of a different gender
   or culture to your own.
   To further develop your communication skills.
   We use *differing* communication skills with our friends and with others we are not
   as close to.
   To develop new friendships.

4. IN **ATTAINMENT LEVEL** GROUPS
   Each one of us is better at some things than at other things. During
   these times you will be working to improve the things that you find
   most difficult in your learning.
   It is **not** a case of being better or worse than others in the class. It is about having,
   in some things, **different needs** for achieving your very best in our subject.

Swapping

Partners

Begin applying A THIRD, A THIRD, A THIRD by simply swapping partners. Lesson one they sit boy, girl. Lesson two they sit with a friend (this will, of course, be single gender!). Next lesson ask them to sit with someone of the same sex that they haven't yet worked with. When all the boys have worked with each other and all the girls have worked with each other, then ask them to sit with a member of the opposite sex that they haven't worked with. Play it as a challenge with Year 7s (S1):

'You have to find quickly, quietly and safely a new partner by the time that I count backwards to zero. Ten, nine, eight ...'

The numbers game

One useful way to ensure precision in pupil groupings in the classroom is for a department to develop a number system like the one on p.38. You number your form lists and put M for male, F for female. Once you get to know the children, you also assess an attainment level. The numbers on the left now give you access to all possible pairs and groupings in the classroom. The children write their number in the exercise books and gradually you build up a set of acetates of who is going to work with whom during a certain lesson or section of work. The example on p.38 will show how this can work.

Using the numbers game

Form list

Name	Gender	Attainment
1	F	A
2	M	B
3	F	C
4	M	A
5	F	B
6	F	A
7	M	B
8	M	C
9	F	B
10	M	B
11	F	A
12	M	A
13	F	A
14	M	B
15	F	C
16	M	C
17	M	A
18	M	B
19	F	B
20	M	C
21	M	C
22	M	A
23	F	A
24	F	B
25	M	B
26	M	A
27	F	A
28	M	A

Acetate example

To assemble the pupils into single-gender attainment level pairings:

(AF)* 1+6   11+13   23+27
(BF)   5+9   19+24
(CF)   3+15
(AM)   4+12   17+22   26+28
(BM)   2+7   10+14   18+25
(CM)   8+20   16+21

Put it on the OHP and count backwards whilst they find their partners.

* It is unhelpful and unnecessary for the whole class to know each other's attainment level, so keep this column covered when displaying the acetate.

Pair work into group work

Groups of four

The best size of a working group is four (an exception to 'going for five'!). When you have five in the group, it is easy for one pupil to take a 'back seat' whilst the others engage. I have noticed that with four to a group, if one tries to opt out then the others will get him or her working again.

Always go through a pair work step in your lesson and then join up the pairs to form your small groups. This way you will find that the groups get better and all children participate more equally in the task. The group is now two sets of pairs rather than four individuals thrown cold into the activity.

To ensure variety and to improve their learning, all children need access to the following:

- Single-gender Attainment Level Groups
- Mixed-gender Attainment Level Groups
- Single-gender Mixed Attainment Level Groups
- Mixed-gender Mixed Attainment Level Groups

A department can ensure this access by developing a planner for specific programmes of study …

PLAN IT!

Department policy guideline

- To develop pupil relationships within the classroom.
- To develop core skills development.
- To improve the oracy and reflective skills of boys.
- To improve the speculative skills and assertiveness of girls.

One-third of group work will be in friendship groupings.
One-third will be in non-friendship single-gender groupings.
One-third will be in mixed-gender groupings.

The groupings will also ensure that all pupils work in attainment and mixed attainment groups periodically and appropriately.

Year 7 schema

Programme of Study

Teaching/Learning	*Ratio: 1/4*
Individual/Proximal	*Ratio: 1/3*
Differentiation by task	*Ratio: 1/12*

(I explain the above ratios in Chapter 7.)

Week no. 1

Lesson 1	Individual Work
Lesson 2	Single-gender Mixed Attainment Groupings
Lesson 3	Mixed-gender Mixed Attainment Groupings
Lesson 4	Friendship Groups

Week no. 2

Lesson 1	Mixed-gender Mixed Attainment Groupings
Lesson 2	Friendship Groups
Lesson 3	Single-gender Mixed Attainment Groupings
Lesson 4	Individual Work

Week no. 3

Lesson 1	Individual Work
Lesson 2	Friendship Groups
Lesson 3	Single-gender Attainment Groupings
Lesson 4	Single-gender Attainment Groupings

Week no. 4

Lesson 1	Individual Work
Lesson 2	Friendship Groups
Lesson 3	Mixed-gender Attainment Groupings
Lesson 4	Mixed-gender Attainment Groupings

TEACH IT!

Children (and adults!) need to be taught how to work in teams. On the following pages are some multi-adaptable ideas to help you to teach the children to listen to and to share ideas with one another.

Adapt the processes to the lesson content and use them for a few minutes just before your group work task. You will find that the pupils work together much better.

Group work development ideas

It is a good idea to practise the method itself, briefly, before using the process technique on the lesson content. So underneath each, in italics, I suggest an entertaining 'way in' to teaching the process:

The basic brainstorm

Everyone quickly calls out ideas. These are not discussed: just written up by one group member.

What are the similarities between a cat and a refrigerator?

The structured brainstorm

Everyone calls out ideas <u>in turn</u> around the circle. Everyone must contribute something. No argument or discussion is allowed.

What would happen if gravity stopped for ten seconds each and every day?

'Around the group in turn' is especially good as a starting activity to get everyone involved in a discussion.

That's important because ...

The affirmation brainstorm (Stage one)

Prior to making his or her own contribution, each child must affirm the previous one that has been made.

Boys will be banned from school unless ...

Example:
Pupil One: Boys will be banned from school unless they learn to listen better.
Pupil Two: That's important because if you don't listen then you won't know what to do. Boys will be banned from school unless they behave better.
Pupil Three: That's important because ...

The affirmation brainstorm (Stage two)

After one participant presents an idea, he or she then points to another member of the group *at random,* who must first affirm this idea before presenting a new one.

The affirmation system, especially in sequence, is very useful in getting pupils to listen to one another's ideas and thus actively to teach listening skills. The problem with group work discussion is that we are so intent on working out what we want to say that we don't really listen to other people's contributions. Here the children have to because another participant's idea is their starting point.

The Pros, Cons, and Interesting Points method	Each person in the group decides on a role and, regardless of personal opinions, must argue in that role. Pros must argue for the idea, Cons against and Interesting Points people merely reflect upon the issue (amusingly perhaps!) without coming down either for or against it. Again, go around the group in turn. No other arguments are allowed! Swap roles after first and second rounds.

It would be better to live life backwards, being born aged 75 and gradually getting younger rather than older!

This is especially good for teaching reflective thinking skills and thus is an especially good activity for boys. It is also useful to get pupils to explore alternative viewpoints to their own. They might have to argue against something they agree with, for example, and thus see things from another perspective.

Courtroom

One person defends an idea, another attacks it. The other two are the judges. They are not allowed to express an opinion but have to ask lots of questions. The judges then make the final decision.

Let's all leave school now and go to the seaside!

This is good for getting people to practise speaking in support of and against ideas. It is especially good for action planning.

Metaphor (Stage one)

Before telling the group the subject for discussion, ask each to think of a noun (any object or animal will do).

Tell them to go around the group and say what their chosen word is.

Introduce your theme and tell the group that they are to use their noun as a metaphor for the subject and to explain it. For example, the word 'building' has been chosen and your theme of 'change'. Then the pupil must begin his or her sentence 'Change is a building because ...' and complete the idea.

This idea is useful for developing creative thinking.

Metaphor (Stage two)

The group chooses one metaphor and everyone explains it in turn.

Pictorial metaphor/simile

The teacher chooses an appropriate pictorial metaphor for the conceptual elements of a lesson.

Each group is given an A3 photocopy of the picture (or different pictures). Working in a group, they then annotate it or adapt it to explore the concept.

Here's a drawing of a house ... show me how this is like the way a baby grows up.

Abstract shopping

Around the group in turn, each pupil says 'I went to the shops to buy' and inserts a concept, skill or consideration rather than an object.

In order to get on well with other people I went to the shops to buy ... tolerance!

Character roles

Each person in turn adopts a character and relates what *this person* would say or think about an issue, for example Mum, Dad, Teacher.

About you not doing your homework!

Relevance

Finally, of course, before you do anything with children, communicate the relevance: tell them *why* you are doing it.

The ideas above are designed for the following reasons:

- To help pupils, especially boys, to develop their communication and group work skills.
- To facilitate everyone being comfortable about making a contribution. This is achieved through creating common structures/rules under which everyone operates: especially when the added rule of 'no argument' is enforced.
- To help especially the boys to develop their listening skills. Again the structures help, especially in the affirmation brainstorms and in the in-role brainstorms: the former helping to create empathy and the latter generating additional interest through the character being played.
- For fun! To illustrate that sharing views and ideas can be fun as well as being important to our own understandings and our understanding of others.

Chapter 5

Descriptive–Reflective–Speculative

Sequence teaching, learning and communication

This is probably the most pedagogically difficult chapter in the entire book! Some homework on the ideas will reward the reader so I'll set you some at the end!

Use Descriptive–Reflective–Speculative sequencing regularly to deliver your lessons. This facilitates the delivery of a really excellent lesson, which (no surprise now to the reader!) has five key components to it.

The excellent lesson

The excellent lesson is a challenging lesson, with clearly defined learning objectives, taught to the top of the class (the highest level of attainment) rather than the middle. It enables sequentially extending times on task rather than block timing. It balances the more formal teaching aspects with the pupils consolidating their learning at each step through 'doing'. It allows for appropriate differentiation by task. And the excellent lesson facilitates the pupils presenting their gains in understandings.

The excellent lesson will have between three and five steps to it. Less than three steps and the teacher will probably not satisfy the needs of the average learner and, almost certainly, fail with the lower attainer. More than five steps and it is likely to be too 'bitty' and lack cohesion. Here's the plan that I shall then explain step by step …

The excellent lesson plan

- Communicate the CHALLENGE
- Communicate the RELEVANCE
- Communicate the GAINS IN LEARNING

Step one: Descriptive activity
              Teach descriptively

Step two: Reflective activity
              Teach reflectively

Step three: Speculative activity
              Teach speculatively

Step four: Central learning activity

Step five: Pupils present their understandings

Debrief gains in learning

Now let me show you how the lesson satisfies the five tenets of excellence. I shall use the example of the Year 9 (S3) lesson on drugs that I cited in Chapter 1. This approach is also applicable in Key Stage 4 and within all subject areas.

An example of an excellent lesson

COMMUNICATE THE CHALLENGE
COMMUNICATE THE RELEVANCE
COMMUNICATE THE GAINS IN LEARNING

You are going to find today's lesson difficult. You will be able to do it but you are really going to have to think deeply and communicate well with others.

Drug taking is an issue that in some way is likely to affect us all.

Today you are going to learn lots of new things about drugs – things you really ought to know if you are to make sensible decisions for yourself.

Step one
DESCRIPTIVE ACTIVITY
TEACH DESCRIPTIVELY

I am going to give you and your partner just one sheet of paper between you. You have just five minutes. Talking with one another, write down ten things you would think of as being drugs. Go.

Well done.

Let me tell you now what the law says an 'Unlawful Substance' is. Listen carefully because your next task is to tick quickly the things on your list that are Unlawful Substances.

Two minutes … go quickly down your list and tick the Unlawful Substances on it.

Step two   REFLECTIVE ACTIVITY
                           TEACH REFLECTIVELY

Now take one of the Unlawful Substances that you ticked. Draw a column down the page. With your partner, and this is really difficult … can you think of five good things and five bad things about this drug?

Let me now take a drug that is readily available and give you some information about its good and bad effects.

Step three   SPECULATIVE ACTIVITY
                           TEACH SPECULATIVELY

As a final task in this part of the lesson, with your partner, select one of the bad effects from your list. Talk about how just this one bad effect might lead on to other consequences. For example, I saw that some of you have written that some drugs can be addictive. If someone is addicted to a drug, can you find five ways that this addiction might affect their lives?

Let me tell you now what some people say are the bad social effects of drug taking.

Step four   CENTRAL LEARNING ACTIVITY

With your partner, join up with another pair to form a group of four. In your group, you are going to explore one of three important issues on which I am going to ask you to report back to the class. You have just 15 minutes to complete your assignment before telling us what you have discovered.

Task One: Here's some information about marijuana. You have to tell us some facts about this drug and tell us why the drug is popular.
(FOR LOW ATTAINERS: DESCRIPTIVE AND EXTEND TO REFLECTIVE – see p.48)

Task Two: A girl goes to a Rave and takes Ecstasy. Why does she do it? If she is going to do it, is there a way she could make sure that she does it more safely? Here's some information about the drug and about drug safety. In 15 minutes' time, you will be telling us your findings.
(FOR AVERAGE ATTAINERS: REFLECTIVE AND EXTEND TO SPECULATIVE)

Task Three: Here's some statistics about drug taking and young people. Find out the 'drugs of preference' for young people of your age, select one, tell us a major problem it causes and tell us some ways we might overcome this problem.
(FOR HIGH ATTAINERS: SPECULATIVE BUT CONSOLIDATE REFLECTIVE)

Step five   PUPILS PRESENT THEIR UNDERSTANDINGS

One group presents. The rest of the class are invited to make comments and ask questions afterwards.

DEBRIEF GAINS IN LEARNING

Well done everyone. Let me conclude by reminding you of some important points from today's lesson ...

Your debrief

Let me now debrief you!

Teaching to the top

Step one starts with the pupils' own understandings. The instruction 'find ten things you would think of as drugs' is challenging. The time is structured and after the five minutes perhaps the highest attainers have found their ten drugs. Perhaps the middle attainers have found seven, and the lowest attainers just three. It doesn't matter! The next instruction draws the class level again: 'select one of your drugs' (one from ten, one from seven, one from three). Everyone in the class has something to take on to the next step.

After 'find five good things and five bad things', the high attainers have maybe five good and five bad, the middle attainers three good things and three bad and the low attainers just one good and one bad. Again it doesn't matter because the next instruction is 'select one of the bad things'.

At each step the class is brought level but all children are extended through the important hierarchy of Descriptive–Reflective–Speculative.

The low attainer needs to extend his or her thinking skills from being simply descriptive. The mid range attainer needs to enhance and develop his or her reflective skills and, together with the low attainer, needs to extend thinking into the speculative dimension. The pair work triggers the proximal learning and the children help one another to think and communicate through this mutually extending process.

And remember that boys especially need to develop their reflective skills.

Sequentially extending times on task

D–R–S is a highly useful system for naturally extending the task time as the lesson progresses. Descriptive activities take the least time, reflective activities longer and speculative ones longer still. The first task facilitated short, quick involvement with immediate outcomes, that is: immediate gratification for the boys!

Notice, as well, how the lesson developed the group work through a pair work step.

The timings?

Step one: 5 minutes.
Step two: 7 minutes.
Step three: 11 or so minutes.
Step four: 15 minutes.
Step five: 20 minutes.

Teaching and doing

At each step in the lesson, there is a learning element taught at precisely the correct moment for it to be understood and, indeed, remembered.

The class is thinking descriptively and then the teacher extends their thinking by teaching descriptively.

By descriptive, I mean what something is or how to do something.

The class then thinks reflectively and then the more reflective learning element is introduced. The analysis is presented to minds ready to receive it!

By reflective, I mean why something is as it is or why I do what I do in the way that I do it.

Speculative thinking is 'if'.

By speculative activities, I mean: if I know what something is or how to do something and I know why this something is how it is or why I do what I do then how can I apply this understanding to the new concept or approach?

I'll leave you to grapple with and speculate upon that last definition!

Differentiation

The drugs lesson illustrates another use for D–R–S: to differentiate by task. Effective differentiation by task is about giving groups appropriate tasks that, within the same time span, deliver similar gains in learning.

An example might be that in technology in Key Stage 3, the pupils who are good at circuitry are given a complicated circuit diagram to make a badge which flashes. The pupils who are weaker at building circuits get a simpler circuit diagram to make a badge which flashes. Everyone leaves with a badge which flashes and everyone has their knowledge of circuitry appropriately extended. The outcome is similar but the task is different.

For low attainer think 'descriptive and extend to reflective'. For mid attainer think 'reflective and extend to speculative'. For high attainer think 'speculative but consolidate their reflective understandings'.

You now have a highly useful and effective coda for devising appropriate tasks.

There is no need to take the labels too literally. You will find that a broad understanding of these terms and the sequence will suffice in helping to plan your lessons.

Presenting back

This lesson has three learning components rather than just one because of the three differing tasks that are set. In presenting back, the pupils are required to communicate their new understandings. To do this, they have to put them in order and to express them clearly and concisely. You are thus helping the boys to develop their linear process skills. In reporting back to the class what they have learnt, the pupils are learning through teaching. And the pupils are teaching one another. You can now assess their gains in learning.

How to plan

Think D–R–S and you have a template for planning some highly dynamic and challenging lessons.

A final point. Plan backwards! Think, what are my gains in learning for this lesson? Next think of a really interesting group work activity to realise these gains. And now think 'how am I going to get the class prepared for this group work activity?' Answer … through three pair-work steps: in turn, descriptive, reflective and speculative.

Homework

Select a key lesson that you are soon to teach. Plan it and deliver it using the Excellent Lesson as a guide.

Action writing and action reading

Writing

We learn nothing BY writing. Writing expresses previous understanding. For writing to be effective in learning, the understanding needs to precede it. Just as oracy precedes literacy, so should thinking and understanding precede writing. Thus writing becomes a tool for expressing and consolidating learning. Boys have weaker verbal skills than girls. Boys have poorer reflective skills than girls. Boys find the dynamics of writing more difficult and writing may actually become a block to their learning. Consider a boy with poor literacy skills. He spends so much time thinking about the formation of words and sentences that he may easily lose the threads of the ideas he is trying to communicate on the page. To so many boys, writing becomes a boring, passive chore that they are forced into doing. The fun of a learning activity may be easily spoilt by having to write it up. Of course, writing is highly important and, with a little imagination and the enactment of the tenets previously explored, writing too may become more boy-friendly as a learning activity.

I remind you of some previously made points. Structure on-task talk. If something is talked through prior to it being written, it is written and understood better. So, as part of your varied diet of activities in the classroom, structure time so that pupils talk through their gain in learning at the end of the lesson prior to writing it down. Writing as a tool for learning should follow the sequence THINK–COMMUNICATE–WRITE. Now, here are some ideas especially appropriate to boys' learning styles that you will find improve the quality of their writing …

Deconstruct it

Think of written language as a system and the word or sentence as an object and you are into the boys' territory. Big words, like facts, are appealing to the male intellect! So, firstly, develop a 'hit list' of key words in your subject and find ways to get pupils playing with these words so that they learn them and can use them appropriately.

- Have quizzes more frequently – five of these key words and their meanings learnt for homework and a quick quiz the following day.
- Have word searches with these key words available for fill-ins at the end of the lesson.
- Introduce new words by a quick word search activity at the start of the lesson. You will find this especially motivating for the boys.
- As you read to the class, ask them to listen out for key words and expressions and to make a quick note of them.
- Before they write, put some words and expressions on the board and instruct the class to use them in what they write.
- Use the 'that is' technique:

'When you use the words that I have put on the board you have to explain them simply, ask your partner to help … Today we learnt about osmosis, that is … '

- Use flashcards and posters. Devise a poster in the form of a diagram with your key words and put it on the wall. Challenge individual pupils to come to the front of the class, point to a word and explain it.
- Boys, especially, like writing on the board, so challenge pupils to come up and write these important words in front of the class.
- Play memory challenges and adding games with your subject's vocabulary.

'Partner A says a word, B repeats it and adds another word, then A repeats both the words and adds a third, and so on. Let's see who gets the longest list of these important words!'

From words to sentences

After actively teaching the words of your subject, develop from phrase stems through sentence stems into paragraph stems. Let me show you what I mean by using the desert island and the mirror example from Chapter 2.

'With your partner, see if you can find five uses of a mirror for survival on a desert island, here … use this sheet to write your ideas down … you have just two minutes!'

1. To _____
2. To _____
3. To _____
4. To _____
5. To _____

The word 'to' requires them to use the verb stem and to write down the participle appropriately: 'to signal' rather than just a single word response 'signalling'.

Now, as I ask you to tell me your ideas, use the word 'to' in your reply and answer me in a short sentence. I am asking you to do this because it helps you to express your ideas better, especially when you come to writing them on paper. OK John ... tell us one of your uses for this mirror.
John: To signal.
Make it a sentence, John ...' You ...'
John: You could use a mirror to signal.
Well done! Good idea!

See what I mean? Having been through this precise deconstructional and verbal process, when they come to write about the desert island and mirror, their written expression will improve considerably and they will remember the ideas better as well.

The next step in this process gives you a very simple and effective way of extending the pupils' writing.

Teach linking words

'Now I want you to select one of your survival uses of a mirror and find five steps for using it. Write your steps down on this sheet ...'

First	_____ .
Secondly	_____ .
Next	_____ .
Then	_____ .
Finally	_____ .

'Well done. Now, as I ask you for your five steps, you have to respond in a full paragraph using the linking words on your sheet. John ... give it a try ... how would you use a mirror to signal?'
'First, you go to high ground. Secondly, you flash the mirror at the sun. Next, you look to see if the ship has seen it. Then you use code to send a message. Finally, you look for instructions.'
'Excellent, well done!'

And well done teacher! With verbal expression preceding written expression you have taught John <u>how</u> to write.

You will find 'first, secondly, next, then and finally' a very effective tool to develop boys' extended writing and also to teach them to sequence things.

Other effective tools

If you wish to get them to illustrate, teach them to use:

> *compared with*
> *in the same way*
> *equally*
> *similarly*
> *as well as*

If you wish to get them to contrast, teach them to use:

> *however*
> *but*
> *on the one hand, on the other*
> *yet*
> *although*

If you wish to get them to persuade:

> *obviously*
> *of course*
> *clearly*
> *surely*
> *certainly*

To give an opinion:

> *it would seem that*
> *possibly*
> *maybe*
> *perhaps*
> *definitely*

To write about cause and effect, then:

> *thus*
> *as a result of*
> *so therefore*
> *because*
> *in order to*

To conclude a piece of writing teach them the words they need to close it:

> *in conclusion*
> *finally*
> *in the end*
> *on the whole*
> *in summary*

Boys especially need to be shown how to use writing as a tool!

Teach D–R–S
You will find that actively teaching especially boys how to write will deliver excellent results. A good piece of written work will follow the sequence Descriptive–Reflective–Speculative just like a good lesson. Teach the class to use the hierarchy. I advocate the use of a classroom poster and / or a printed copy of *Action writing* given on p.54 for each child that ever has to write anything!

— Action writing —

Use
DESCRIPTIVE
REFLECTIVE
SPECULATIVE

First
Describe the scene
Explain the facts
Explain the sequence or steps in doing something

Then
Explain the feelings
Explain the consequences
Explain the result

Finally
Draw conclusions
Present new ideas
Speculate upon possibilities

THINK, COMMUNICATE AND WRITE D–R–S!

Reading

For writing to enrich learning, the sequence is Think–Communicate–Write.
Reading as a tool for learning follows the sequence READ–THINK–
COMMUNICATE.

Girls and boys tend to read quite differently. Boys read material directly related to their interests and, broadly speaking, for the purpose of acquiring information and factual detail. Girls will read anything as long as it is about people and their relationships! Girls read from start to finish whilst boys 'skip read' even to the extent of starting the book at chapter five. If a boy is getting bored, he will readily miss a few pages and jump to a bit he finds more interesting. He is more likely to skim the book first and be drawn into reading through pictures and diagrams. I suspect that the bedside table of most men will hold three books: one on politics, a biography or similar book related to their interests and a travel book. Their shelves are likely to be filled by books that have been partly read!

With boys especially, it is important for the teacher to give them a clear brief. Tell them why you are asking them to read a particular thing and define a purpose for the reading. The more precise you can make it, the better for the pupils.

Reading for purpose

Ask pupils to read for the purpose of finding information which they are then going to use:

'You have ten minutes to read chapter one on the causes of the Second World War. Quickly jot down any information you find on industry and territory. Then select five important details from your list. I'm then going to ask you to tell me what they are and to explain why you think they are important pieces of information.'
(DESCRIPTIVE–REFLECTIVE).

Reinforcement

Periodically, prior to the introduction of new content, get the pupils to read to consolidate the things that they have learnt so far:

'Firstly, I want you to read, in pairs and in turn to one another, the way that Hans asked Gita the way to the station, then we will be finding some new ways of giving people directions.'

Incorporate more of this type of reading activity in Key Stage 4.

Interaction through speculation

Meaning and understanding are syntheses of what the writer writes and the reader or learner brings to the text him or herself. With boys, it is important to activate overtly this relationship. Think speculate and you have a boy-friendly reading activity:

'Read just paragraph one and then turn your book over. Given our analysis of the character, how do you think she is likely to react?'
'Given what you have just read about the chemicals involved, what do you think will happen when they are combined?'

Don't give them the answer, instead:

'Now read on and discover whether or not you are correct.'

Or, for example:

'As you read about Jane, imagine that you are her! When you get to the end of the page, stop reading and jot down a few words to describe how you would feel in Jane's position.'
'Looking at the map of Europe in 1945, what do you think will be the major problems in the following decade?'

55

Read to record information

Provide headings on the board or a worksheet and instruct the pupils to make word notes under each heading as they read:

'Read chapter one about France for homework and make notes under the headings on your worksheet. Tomorrow you are going to be travellers returning from the country and you are going to be interviewed on television about what you have learnt from your trip.'

And go for five!

Teach this approach as a study / revision skill in KS4.

Study notes

Country: _____

The terrain
1.
2.
3.
4.
5.

The climate
1.
2.
3.
4.
5.

The people
1.
2.
3.
4.
5.

The exports
1.
2.
3.
4.
5.

The imports
1.
2.
3.
4.
5.

Critical reading

Reading can become a significant way to extend boys' reflective thinking skills.

'As you read this piece, use your worksheet to jot down some ways in which you agree with the writer and some ways in which you disagree. See if you can find five points of agreement and five points of disagreement. Later, we will be using this sheet to have a full-scale debate on the issues.'

'One of you read the chapter to your group. Whilst you are listening to the reader, one of you note down some arguments against what the writer is saying. Another note down ways in which the writer is showing bias. The fourth, see if you can find examples of the way in which the writer is being sexist!'

'Read the section in turn around the group and then, as a group, see if you can find five things that you disagree with.'

Reading to teach

Many boys like to show off! Capitalise upon it and you have a neat way of covering a lot of information quickly:

'This is an activity called EXPERTS. It works like this: you have just 15 minutes each to read a different section of the book and make notes. Then you are going to become the expert and teach the rest of your group what you have discovered. They are then going to take notes from you and in this way everyone will have learnt a lot.'

'I'm going to divide the class up into six groups. Each group is going to have a different section/chapter to read. Each group should read their section taking turns and then make one set of notes on it. Then, in turn, you are going to teach the class about your section, whilst they, in their turn, take notes.'

This process is a highly effective way of covering curriculum content in KS4.

Paired reading

Rather than you reading to the class, think 'Is there an opportunity here to develop literacy skills?' Pupils reading quietly to one another in pairs is an excellent way to improve their skills. Begin this process when they are young and by getting them to read their *own homework* to one another. If a child is writing something for the purpose of reading it to another child, he or she will take more care over the piece of work. As well as consolidating the learning in reading to one another, they will also be correcting any mistakes they find. Add the 'experts' idea where the listening partner makes notes and you are on to a real motivational winner with boys!

Remember also that it doesn't matter a jot what children read as long as they do read! With boys especially, if they are interested in a specific topic, then this may be used with great effect to develop their interest and skills in reading itself. Literacy skills development is not the responsibility of the English department. It is a cross-curricular imperative. The best results in developing reading and writing skills with boys who find it difficult will come in boy-friendly areas of the curriculum. Hit literacy skills development through science and technology! And use a varied approach so that all children within a certain time frame have all the reading opportunities possible. Here they are!

Variety check-list

Action	Purpose	Interaction
Teacher reads to class	Reinforcement To speculate To be critical To record information For fun	Pupils follow Pupils make notes
Pupils read to one another in pairs Pupils read their homework to one another in pairs	Reinforcement To speculate To be critical To record information For fun	Listener makes notes Pair to teach other pair Pair to teach class
One pupil read to small group Pupils read in turn around the group	Reinforcement To speculate To be critical To record information For fun	Listeners make notes together and prioritise Each listener has something specific to listen for Groups teach class
Individual pupils read to class (good readers only!)	Reinforcement To speculate To be critical To record information For fun	All make notes Groups listen out for specifics

Out-loud reading

Reading out loud is a fine way to develop reading skills. To encourage boys to read out loud, be it their own work or from a book, first ask them to read to one another in pairs. It is also a good idea to give them some time to rehearse their readings prior to reading out loud. A useful homework assignment, for example, could be to practise reading a section of a book out loud because next lesson they will be reading it to the class.

Reading skills

Take some time, especially in Key Stage 4, actively to teach reading strategies. Introduce and teach the skills involved through high challenge games. Teach your pupils *to scan* for specific information by running their fingers down the right-hand side of the page and looking for certain words. When they see a word, tell them to read the sentence that contains it. Teach them how *to skim* for gist by running their fingers along the lines quickly, stopping and recalling the information they have taken in. And teach them occasionally to read intensively by holding their book up in front of them and reading every word.

Try teaching them to punctuate accurately by asking them at times to say 'comma, full stop', and so on whilst they read.

Reading and writing proportions

Some 18 to 20% of classroom time should be used in reading in a variety of ways. Some 20 to 25% of time should be used in writing in a variety of ways. One sees far too little reading and way too much writing!

Start thinking RATIOS ...

Chapter

7

Teach how, think ratios

Using classroom time more effectively

How often do you think that Darren says to his mates 'Hey guys, let's all go down the corner and analyse a poem?' Probably not a lot.

A great deal of learning is not rational, it is logical. So much of what we try to teach boys runs counter-intuitive and contrary to their nature. It needs to be taught. This is an important point so I will press it. You need to be taught if you are to learn. Let me give an example of the counter-intuitive nature of learning and the necessity for an 'up-front' approach to teaching.

Which door?

Imagine you are taking part in a Game Show on television. The game host shows you three doors and she says to you 'I know what's behind each of these doors and you don't. Behind two of them is a cabbage. Behind the third is a million pounds. Choose a door!'

You then select but are not allowed to open one of the doors.

She then opens one of the doors that you haven't chosen and reveals a cabbage behind it. 'Would you like to change your mind?' she now says, 'If you wish to, you can now choose the last door instead of your original one.'

Assuming you don't actually wish to win the cabbage, the question is: should you now change your original choice to the last door? Do you stand more chance of winning the million pounds that way? Think about it before you read on.

The answer is at the end of the chapter. You were probably wrong.

Why were you wrong? Probability is logical not rational. The mathematical reality of the world we live in runs counter-intuitive. We call our failure to grasp probability theory 'Sod's Law'. In a supermarket, you are always in a slow queue. Well, you will be. Five queues and you choosing just one only gives you a one in five chance of being in the fastest. Your own personal, rational and intuitive world has no real need to understand the subtleties of probability mathematics. You would probably never rationally come up with the reasons behind its laws or, indeed, find it easy to accept that, through changing your choice of door, you double your chances of being a millionaire. It has to be taught to you. Darren needs to be taught poetry analysis.

'Reader, if you ever take part in a Game Show and are shown three doors and later a cabbage behind one of them, then given the choice, change your first decision.'

'Class, here is a poem and my five steps of how to analyse it. Let me take you through each step and show you how it is done. Now, here's another poem. Using my steps, see if you can crack the code of this poem. Work in mixed pairs. You have ten minutes, the clock starts now!'

Teach how before why

In maths, the numbers define the concept. To understand the concepts of probability you have first to know how to use number. Thus learning works in many spheres. If you wish to understand what caused the First World War, you need to be taught how to understand it first through the application of cause and effect. Conceptual understanding fails if we do not give pupils the language and thinking tools to understand it. Boys especially relate well to this kind of learning skills-based training. 'This is how to think, now think this way in order to understand!'

In simple terms in the classroom, this means TEACH HOW BEFORE WHY. Teach Descriptive before Reflective. I remind you of the excellent lesson in Chapter 5. The Descriptive is what something is or HOW to do something. Look at one of your programmes of study. Think of the key 'hows' in it and teach them overtly and sequentially using D–R–S and you will see a major improvement in your boys' performance and *motivation*.

After all, I am likely to have little interest in knowing why I do what I can't do in the first place!

Ratios

There are four key ratios in learning management:

TEACHING TO DOING
INDIVIDUAL TO PROXIMAL
UNDIFFERENTIATED TO DIFFERENTIATED
PRAISE TO REPRIMAND

The Teaching to Doing ratio is the proportion of time a teacher spends teaching the whole class to the amount of time the pupils spend on-task. The Individual to Proximal ratio is the amount of on-task time spent working individually to the amount of time spent working in a structured way in pairs or groups. The Differentiation ratio is how much time needs to be given to activities which are differentiated by task. And the Praise to Reprimand ratio is, and must never drop below, 3:1. More about this aspect in the next chapter.

Teaching to doing

In order to teach the many hows demanded in learning, the teaching to doing ratio needs to be pretty high. By teaching, I mean interactive and dynamic, step-by-step approaches such as illustrated in Chapter 5. As a broad rule of thumb, I give some examples below of how much time the teacher needs to teach in Key Stage 3. The first part of the ratio refers to the amount of time the teacher spends addressing the whole class and the second, the amount of time the pupils are engaged in a *wide variety* of tasks.

MATHS	1 : 1
MODERN LANGUAGES	1 : 3
ENGLISH	1 : 4
HISTORY	1 : 3
GEOGRAPHY	1 : 3
SCIENCE	1 : 5
TECHNOLOGY	1 : 5

Individual to proximal

There are two ways that children learn: on their own and together with other children. Thus the doing part of the ratio on the right above is then broken down into these two types of doing.

	TEACHING		INDIVIDUAL		PROXIMAL
MATHS	1	/ :	0.5	:	0.5
MOD. LANG.	1	/ :	1	:	2
ENGLISH	1	/ :	1	:	3
HISTORY	1	/ :	1	:	2
GEOGRAPHY	1	/ :	1	:	2
SCIENCE	1	/ :	2	:	3
TECHNOLOGY	1	/ :	1	:	4

Differentiation by task

This is the number of lessons that should be differentiated through group work by giving *differing* tasks appropriate to the pupils' attainment levels.

Differentiation by task is the only useful form of differentiation.

Differentiation by outcome is largely bad practice! Differentiation by outcome would be each group, regardless of attainment level, being given the same task. In the lower attaining group, there would, of course, be far more boys than girls! So here goes. The number of lessons with an average class you should be looking to differentiate in this way:

MATHS	1 in every 12 or so
MODERN LANGUAGES	1 in every 15 or so
ENGLISH	1 in every 20 or so
HISTORY	1 in every 10 or so
GEOGRAPHY	1 in every 15 or so
SCIENCE	1 in every 10 or so
TECHNOLOGY	1 in every 10 or so

Notice a degree of vagueness seeping in? You know your pupils and your subject. My aim is to challenge your analysis. The ratio system is a tool for encouraging teachers to be a little more precise in translating pedagogy into classroom practice. Make your own decision about what these ratios should be but THINK RATIOS and you have a tool for improving pupils' performance. Here are the Equal Opportunities guidelines:

Equal opportunities

If there is too much teaching and not enough doing then the boys are likely to be turned off. If there is too little teaching and too much doing then the girls are likely to be disadvantaged. A balance needs to be struck. If too much of the doing is individual doing then you disadvantage the pupils with weaker doing skills (especially writing and reading skills), ironically perhaps the boys. The boys are great at doing their own thing but not so hot at doing the logical learning things!

Effective Differentiation is best undertaken towards the end of a programme of study and not at its start. Such tasks are better to consolidate and extend understanding rather than to initiate it. The how should precede the why, so new learning should be initiated through lots of high quality, whole-class teaching. And here is a final point, which I believe is relevant to include here. When you are engaging in your high quality *teaching* ratio and the children are consolidating through their *individual* learning ratio, make more use of diagrams. Boys with their much better visuo-spatial skills will understand and learn things better if they can apply this strength in girl-friendly arenas such as English. It will also help girls to simplify their ideas.

Key Stage 4

In Key Stage 4, the emphasis shifts towards the doing rather than the teaching side of the ratio and ideally towards more individualised learning rather than group work differentiation. However, there remains a strong imperative for continuing sequential, step-by-step, whole-class teaching. Thus the time ratios might look something like this:

Teaching to doing

MATHS	1 : 3
MODERN LANGUAGES	1 : 5
ENGLISH	1 : 6
HISTORY	1 : 6
GEOGRAPHY	1 : 6
SCIENCE	1 : 8
TECHNOLOGY	1 : 8

Individual to proximal

	TEACHING		INDIVIDUAL		PROXIMAL
MATHS	1	/:	2	:	1
MOD. LANG.	1	/:	2	:	3
ENGLISH	1	/:	3	:	3
HISTORY	1	/:	4	:	2
GEOGRAPHY	1	/:	4	:	2
SCIENCE	1	/:	4	:	4
TECHNOLOGY	1	/:	4	:	4

My impression is that pupils at Key Stage 4, generally speaking, are not getting enough whole-class teaching and certainly (from the boys' perspective) not enough proximal learning.

Solution to which door?

The answer to the problem is if you change your original choice to the last door remaining then you *double* your chances of winning the million pounds!

When you selected one of the doors you had a one in three chance of winning the million pounds. (Your rational thinking and logical thinking are at one.)

The other two doors that you didn't choose each have a one in three chance of having a million pounds behind them. That is, a *combined* probability of two in three. When the Game Show host opens one of these doors to show you a cabbage, the other door left not chosen and unopened must now have a probability of two in three of having the million pounds behind it, since this was the combined probability against you in the first place. (Your rational thinking is probably now at odds with your logical thinking!)

Conceptual understanding in maths, as I have pointed out, only comes through number. The numbers define the concepts. Being able to rationalise mathematics is dependent upon the logical process skill of number operation. Being able to rationalise learning content is similarly bound to the logical process skill of thought operation and application (thinking skills). In maths, we must teach children first how to think mathematically, in science, scientifically, and so on. Think about it. Perhaps a diagram will help!

Diagram

---

* your choice, # door opened by host after your choice, £ million pounds

DOOR	A		B	C	Change	Don't Change
	*		#	£	WIN	lose
	#		*	£	WIN	lose
	(#)	or	(#)	£*	lose	WIN

Regardless of which door has the million pounds, if you change your original choice you double your chances of winning.

If we teach children HOW to think in subject-specific ways, we double their chance of learning!

Chapter

8

Monitor–Praise–Mentor

Motivating boys and managing their behaviour

There are two types of boy. There is Darren (or Lee, or Clint, or Wayne) and there is Matthew. Have I just fallen into the trap of stereotyping that I took so much time in Chapter 1 to free myself from? Well, not exactly. Teachers throughout the land speak of their troublesome, difficult boys and more frequently than not they are called the former! I remind you that I am not speaking about *all* Darrens or Lees. I remind you, too, of the chicken and egg nature of self-fulfilling prophecy. I shall continue to categorise as above for the purposes of this chapter. I do it tongue-in-cheek. I also do it with affection. There is something about Darren that I find quite endearing!

Darren

Darren is the Alpha Male. He is a cocky, challenging boy who presents teachers with problems in the classroom. He is a high status male within his peer group. Sometimes physically larger that his friends, he is frequently good at sports and good at fighting. There are degrees of 'Darrenness' from the out and out leader of the gang down to the sad, little minor Darren who is easily led into trouble and frequently gets all the blame for it. He is categorised by the remark 'behaviour bad'.

Matthew

Matthew is the quiet lad. He does just enough work to get by but seldom stretches himself. He doesn't get into much trouble. He does his homework, but never too brilliantly. In fact, Matthew drops out quietly and passively. He does it frequently between Year 7 (S1) and Year 8 (S2) and nobody notices very much. Matthew accounts for much of boys' underattainment in school. He is categorised by the remark 'effort poor'.

The point

One thing about boys is that they are pretty easy to categorise and, indeed, stereotype. As a teacher said to me once, 'If you see the name Ricky on your register then watch out, whereas if his parents call him Richard then he will be well behaved.' Given this albeit simplistic categorisation, we can then begin to make use of the information it provides. Labels can fine-tune our thinking down to the individual needs of an individual child. This is how to do it.

Give teachers a class list with tick boxes labelled 'average', 'good', or 'poor' under each of two headings: behaviour and effort. Ask them to tick and this is an example of the outcomes ...

	Effort			Behaviour		
	A	**G**	**P**	**A**	**G**	**P**
Cindy		x			x	
Darren			x			x
Matthew			x		x	

Importantly, you are now getting teachers to notice Matthew where previously they didn't! Then, a couple of hours of secretarial time can transfer all teachers' responses onto a computer database (Microsoft's Excel for example). With a little ingenuity from the IT department, even the largest school will now be able to sort data very quickly. The instruction 'sort/boys/behaviour: poor' will deliver, for example, a list of boys who 50% of teachers have diagnosed to be problematic, that is your Darrens! The instruction sort/boys/effort: poor/behaviour: average' will readily produce a list of your Matthews (regardless of their actual names!). Do this at the end of the Autumn Term in Year 7 (S1), keep doing it regularly and you throw a net that catches your potential problems early. Now you can do something about them proactively. You can simply and effectively begin a process of behaviour modification.

Behaviour modification

We motivate and modify behaviour through PRAISE. It can never be done through sanction or punishment. Punishment might contain behaviour but it will not modify it. For Darren, punishment might even be a reward that secures him prestige in the eyes of his peers. There are numerous examples where sanction slips and the like have actually been collected by boys as merit certificates! It can easily become cool to be disruptive!

Behavioural modification theory dictates that if we want to modify pupils' behaviour then we have to catch them doing things right and praise them for it, and ignore them for the most part when they are doing things wrong.

The untidy child

Let's say, for example, that you have an untidy 11-year-old boy (or girl) in your family. You nag him to be tidy and it doesn't work. You have a row and send him upstairs to tidy his room (you know the sort of thing: 'Don't come down until your room is tidy!'). OK, so he comes down eventually and his room is now tidy. But for how long? Tomorrow it's a mess again because you haven't actually done anything to address the untidy behaviour, you have simply *contained* it.

Using praise

If you wish this child to be consistently tidy then you have to establish the habit of tidiness. To do this you need to catch him being tidy and praise him for it and ignore him when he is being untidy. A major problem! How do you catch him being tidy when he is never, but never, tidy! (This example is actually a gender issue in itself. As referred to previously, men, like boys, tend to miss out steps in doing things. A common one is the 'laundry basket step' between the bedroom floor and the washing machine! Some would say that it is, in fact, a redundant step. These people would mostly be male!) Anyway, back to your untidy 11-year-old. How to catch him being tidy when he never is: well you can't, obviously. But you can do this. Lay off the nagging a little and, for example, say to him at three on a Saturday afternoon, 'Would you help me do something? I'll tell you what ... if you help me do something for half an hour then, at four o'clock, we will go out for a beefburger and milkshake, how does that sound? Would you help me to tidy *my* room?'

You are now in a position where you can show this child how to be tidy. (A fairly obvious reason for untidiness in itself and one likely to be overlooked by the adult is that the child may not actually know HOW to be tidy, or HOW to behave well!) You are also in a position where you heap praise upon the child for helping you. However, you have been just a tad manipulative in this process. At three-thirty, you finish tidying your room and say, 'As promised we'll go out at four. Busy yourself for half an hour!' Now watch that child go up to his room and tidy it! If you don't believe it works then give it a try.

This technique is representative of a behaviour modification technique for boys. Like the untidy 11-year-old, it will not work every time with every child but it will work much of the time with most children. Before I adapt this technique for school let me say two more important things about praise. Check your classroom for who gets praised most and don't be English with it! (See below!)

Praise in the classroom

When you run a check-list on praise in the classroom, you discover, much to the teacher's surprise, that boys actually get much more than girls. The child who is likely to get the most praise is, in fact, the most disruptive boy in that class. The child who gets the least praise in any classroom is likely to be the one who is well behaved and whose work is not excellent. Gifted children get much praise through their work, the average child, however, gets very little praise. That is, the majority of children, in the average classroom, get very little praise indeed! That is patently wrong.

The English and praise

Lecture in the USA and they come up, shake you by the hand, and say, 'I really enjoyed that, lots of good ideas, well done!' In England (not, let me say, Wales or Scotland!) the praise goes like this: 'Thanks, I quite enjoyed that, lots of good ideas ... one small thing I'd like to take you up on ... ' The English do two things with their praise. Firstly, they don't give it enough and secondly, when they do, they diminish it in some way.

One observes these two things in the English classroom. English children don't get enough praise to sustain their motivation. Take, for example, a child putting his or her hand up to answer a question. For many children that is a difficult thing to do. He or she is risking being wrong and risking being laughed at or made fun of. The difficulty of this involvement should always be rewarded by the teacher's praise (even a 'thank you' will do), yet it too frequently isn't. It is taken for granted and participation levels drop because it is taken for granted! Then you observe a teacher going over to Darren. 'An excellent piece of work!' she says and you think 'Well done, you are catching this child doing things right but please STOP THERE!' She doesn't! '... It's a pity you can't work like that all the time!' It's the English way and the effect of the praise is ruined. It is now a reprimand!

IF YOU NEED TO TELL CHILDREN OFF, THEN TELL THEM OFF. IF YOU PRAISE THEM, THEN PRAISE THEM – ONE OR THE OTHER BUT DON'T MIX THE TWO. That deserves emphasis. It is crucial for managing the behaviour of boys. Emphasise another understanding and you are beginning to get powerful tenets for motivating and managing boys in the classroom.

Private rather than public

Boys are highly prone to the influence of their peer group. As a boy grows older, what his mates think about him can become far more important to him than what any adult, parent or teacher alike, thinks about him. Public praise with some boys might actually be counter-productive. Getting your merit certificate at assembly lays you open to being called a swot. It can seriously damage your street cred! He still needs his praise, of course, but he might need it privately rather than publicly. And this is how you do it. It is very un-English but give it a try ...

Catch him doing things right but take him quietly away from his friends at the end of the lesson:

'Darren ... a word ...'

Praise him: *'You've really worked well this lesson. Well done!'*

Remind him of previous <u>good</u> behaviour: *'That's the second time this week you have worked well!'*

Now challenge him: *'Do you think you will be able to work well next lesson?'*

Then communicate your trust in him: *'I think you'll be able to!'*

Finally, seek to reward him for the continuing good work and let him know what is in it for him in the *short* term: *'If you do ...'*

Monitoring–Praising–Mentoring

Now, here is how to use the Monitoring system with the tenets above to deliver some real changes at school. The first step is 'M' for monitoring. Don't sort your database yet for your Darrens and Matthews. Firstly, sort for all children whose behaviour is classified by most teachers as being average or good. Mail-merge a letter home to their parents to credit their good behaviour (something else a database allows you to do easily). In home–school partnership terms, this positive affirmation is well worth the cost of postage. The children who deserve praise are now all getting it.

But poor Darren! He isn't getting his letter home. Now 'M' for mentor.

'Darren, I'd really like you to get a letter posted home to your parents! Here's what we are going to do. Here's a special sheet of paper for you. Collect me ten signatures by tomorrow night and I will send your parents the letter. This is how it works. When you behave well, take it to your subject teachers and ask them to sign it for you. Think you'll be able to get the ten signatures? I think you will … go for it!'

Surprisingly perhaps, this strategy works with many older boys as well. Even the most challenging of Year 10 (S4) and Year 11 (S5) students may be motivated by collecting teacher signatures – if not for a letter home then for some other reward such as, for example, a voucher for sportswear.

Use a similar process to target Matthew and his effort problems. Now you are into behavioural modification, in a simple, down-to-earth and practical way.

Rewards

Merit points

A good merit system is a *proactive* tool for motivation. The Golden Rule for boys is that rewards should come sooner rather than later. Remember, boys have a need for *immediate* gratification. Think 'what are their motivational needs' and use your merit system for *short-term* gains. Take the example of boys (mostly) who fail to bring their pens with them to lessons. A two-week *merit blitz* in Year 7 (S1) and Year 8 (S2) delivers good results on this one.

Just for two weeks, the form tutor checks to see if the pupils have their pens with them at the start of the day. Those that have them are given extra merit points just for this short period of time. Those that don't have them are not punished but simply ignored. You will find at the end of the fortnight that more boys will have their pens. And, significantly, even though they won't be getting merit points anymore for it, they will continue to bring their equipment with them to class. They have now learnt to organise themselves better and started to form better habits. Similar processes may be adopted to good effect on issues such as neatness and punctuality.

Prizes

The best merit systems are cumulative and, for boys especially, *collectable*. For example, ten merit points mean that the pupils will receive a bronze merit certificate *plus* a biro with the school's name on it. Collect 30 merit points and you receive a silver certificate and a pen inscribed with your name, and so on. Tuck shop vouchers and such like are also similarly motivating. Have some big prizes occasionally and you are onto a real winner with boys! 'The first pupil who manages five gold certificates this term will win a Mountain Bike!' Or give raffle tickets along with merit awards to add an element of competition and fun. Most usefully of all, get your student council to decide on the awards and prizes that the pupils in your school would like to receive.

Homework

Never, but never, punish a boy *with work* for not doing his work! Boys readily associate punishment directly with written work. Consider the boy who doesn't do his homework and then ends up in detention doing it. Is he learning anything through this? Little, I suggest, other than working reluctantly avoids punishment. He should positively want to do his homework! Put a time limit on the homework, seek quality rather than quantity and reward a good piece of homework with *double* the merit points to an equivalent piece of classwork and you are now proactively motivating this boy. And *do* question the variety and quality of the homework you set! Finishing off classwork is not a valid activity. Just consider the time gap between when it was started and when completed. Time gap equals learning gap.

Assignment ideas

Here are some good homework assignments especially for boys:

Teach your parents five things that you have learnt this lesson and get them to sign your homework diary when you have done it!

Practise reading this chapter out loud because you will be reading it to one another and answering questions on it in class tomorrow.

Look at the statements on your homework sheet and under each write a short sentence on why the statement is true or false.

Draw a simple diagram that explains ...

Invent five quiz questions about ... and tomorrow you will be asking them to others in the class. Write the answers at the bottom of the page.

In this short piece of writing, I shall just be giving you merit points for correct punctuation and spelling.

I just want you to select and complete five of these sums. But, as well as getting them right, I want you to concentrate on your presentation, ensuring that your sums and their answers are written legibly.

Find me five useful facts about ... and write them out neatly.

Write down five things you would use as evidence in support of this concept that we will be studying in detail next lesson.

If some pupils still don't do their homework, then counsel rather than punish. Find out why. Think about setting up homework clubs or finding a quiet space during the day for an individual child to complete his or her homework. Finally, involve parents sooner rather than later. Suggest that they give their child a little time to help him or her with homework. The best strategy is for parents to take a few minutes with their son or daughter prior to the homework and facilitate its planning. Next, the parent sends the child away for a set time, for example 20 minutes, and asks him or her to return to read or explain the homework to him or her. Now the child should be given lots of praise for it!

Marking

Have you noticed that boys ask you more than girls whether you have marked their worked? Marking is an important tool for motivation. Wean your class off marking out of ten! This form of marking can be demotivating. If someone gave you nine out of ten then the lasting thought is not how good it is but what was wrong with it! We should only mark something down if we can suggest how it might be improved. Any negative comments are useless unless we can suggest exactly and usefully how improvements can be made in the short term.

Reward effort

'Effort' is the most important ingredient in a child's learning success. It is the great Common Denominator. The more able child can, with very little effort, produce a strong piece of work. Merit them on effort rather than attainment and their work will be even better. Reward effort and the less able child may gain a similar number of merit certificates as the most gifted.

Mark work less but mark it more wisely. Make three positive comments about a pupil's work and conclude by setting a target for improvement: *'To improve further, next time ...'*

Finally, end by stating the number of merits the child has received for effort.

Sanctions

Withdrawal of privileges

Boredom is the key to punishment for a boy! A 20-minute detention sitting in silence and doing nothing will seem like an hour to the typical boy. Lunch-time detentions are best of all. You are denying them the game of football with their friends. Generally speaking, however, the withdrawal of privileges is better than punishment.

Take as the example here a typical school rule: NO CHEWING. The most crass of all school rules! It is not actually the chewing which is the major issue. It is what the children do with the chewing gum after they have chewed it that's the problem! I can always tell whether the schools I visit attempt to enforce a chewing ban. If they do then they have the undersides of desks covered with chewing gum! If you want to address underlying behaviour then avoid banning it, tackle this underlying behaviour! Allow chewing at appropriate times (such as during individual work) as long as, after the work is completed, the children remove the gum, wrap it and put it in the bin. Withdraw the privilege if it is abused. You are now into behavioural *modification* again!

School rules

School rules should be few in number and should be aimed at actively teaching the appropriate behaviour. If you cannot explain in 'pupil speak' why the rule is important and you can't use it actively to *praise* pupils then the rule is not worth having. School rules should be phrased positively and become guidelines for the good behaviour they seek to inculcate.

Good and bad rules

A bad school rule:

NO CHEWING

A good school rule:

WE TREAT EVERYONE WITH RESPECT
We do this
by waiting our turn in class;
by not interrupting others when they are speaking;
by being sensitive to the needs of others;
by helping one another to do things;
by helping one another to learn.

Post the good rule up on your classroom wall and then you can discuss it in detail and praise through it: *'Well done for waiting patiently, John. I'll be with you in a moment!'* Try doing that with the NO CHEWING rule!

All too frequently, teachers attempt to use school rules as a control device. Darren comes in late and, rather than just addressing this behaviour, the teacher turns to him and says '... And where's your tie?' Addressing the issue of a child's lateness is much more difficult to us than throwing a rule at the problem or side-stepping the issue by throwing another one at it. The more challenging Darren is, the more the rule is irrelevant to him or the more he will flout it just to seem cool to his mates.

Behaviour is an issue for each individual teacher in his or her own classroom. It is not something that can be managed five hundred feet away by the Head or SMT. School rules and their associated merit systems should be carrots, not sticks to beat children with.

Don't mix

The better your merit system the less you need a demerit system. Motivation and Behaviour Management are all about the separation of powers. Tell or Discuss but don't mix the two. Counsel or Sanction but don't mix the two. Praise or Reprimand but don't mix the two! An example: Matthew is challenged to make improved effort by collecting ten stars in his homework diary for a reward of some kind. He manages to collect nine of them and suddenly his effort flags. We shouldn't take stars away from him. If appropriate then punish him but make sure he knows he has just one more star to collect for the reward.

If you need a demerit system of any kind to keep track of sanctions applied, then ensure that these are kept separate to your system for logging rewards. If pupils use a homework diary, for example, to collect merits then only positive things should go into this diary. As soon as negative remarks or demerits are written in homework diaries, they begin mysteriously to get themselves lost! Would you cherish something that constantly informs you of your failures and weaknesses? On the floor of the motivation market, one demerit trades for four merits. They are expensive little items, handle them with care!

Three to one

Praise versus reprimand

Should we wish to motivate boys or modify their behaviour (as indeed, we should!) then the praise to reprimand ratio must never drop below 3:1 as a bottom line minimum in favour of the former. Ideally it should be four to one, five to one, twenty to one. Or, indeed twenty to zero!

If you shout at a puppy for wetting your carpet, then you have to praise it four times for the more domestically acceptable behaviour in the garden. Better not to shout at it in the first place! We know that moaning at children and punishing them seldom delivers results but we do it anyway!

To classroom-train a typical boy, ensure that you never violate the three to one rule. If you tick every time a teacher praises a class and every time a teacher tells off that class and the ratio drops below three to one, then the teacher is beginning to have major control problems. If you tell off a pupil and you wish him or her to modify his or her behaviour then, after you tell the child off, you must praise the appropriate behaviour at least four times.

Build up the ticks on the praise side of the ratio, try to ignore the negative behaviour whilst praising the positive, and you will quickly deliver the results you want.

And remember, don't be English. 'Well done, Fido, for peeing in the garden. It's a pity you can't pee in the garden all the time!' is a pretty pointless thing to say, isn't it?

Chapter

9 *Assertiveness and the three Rs*

Strategies for managing challenging behaviour

When dealing with challenging behaviour in the classroom from boys especially, we should avoid being aggressive. If we handle aggressive behaviour with aggression, then we are modelling the very same behaviour we wish to counter. *Assertive* behaviour, on the other hand, is calm and honest behaviour. It seeks modification rather than manipulation and conflict resolution rather than containment. It is most certainly not about being passive or weak. Boys and girls relate equally well to an adult who is firm but fair; strict, if you like, but kindly with it.

In this chapter, I suggest some simple strategies for managing behaviour with the more difficult boy in mind. Sorry Darren, you again I'm afraid!

The passing technique

'See me later!' is the Passing Technique. Darren comes in late. Avoid challenging him over his lateness in front of the class. It gives him an opportunity to argue with you. More troublesome boys are excellent at manipulating conflict. Tell them off publicly and you are providing an opportunity for them to *show off* in front of their friends. It might well contain the immediate behaviour but watch out! In demeaning this boy in front of his friends, you are storing up problems for yourself later on in that lesson. He has been 'put down' in front of his friends and he will then seek to build his esteem up again. Turn your back and he will soon be showing off again!

Comment after the lesson

So when Darren comes in late, say 'See me later, Darren!' quietly to him and at the end of the lesson say quietly, although audibly to the rest of the class, 'Remember, Darren, you have to see me before you leave.' The rest of the class will know that you are going to deal with his lateness and Darren now gets a quiet, calm and private word from you. Now separate the powers, tell or discuss, but don't mix the two: 'Darren, don't be late to my lesson again, please!' or 'Why were you late, Darren? Let's talk about it.'

With boys, it is important to deal with things at the end of the lesson rather than, for example, to ask them to see you at break time. Break time means punishment rather than counselling.

76

The private reprimand

Let's assume that badly-behaved Darren, after coming in late, now goes to the corner of the room and starts being a nuisance all over again! Rather than telling him off in front of the class, walk slowly over to him, go down to his level and whisper the reprimand. Make the telling off *behaviour-specific* and separate the child from his mistake: *'Darren stop that, it's stupid behaviour! You are an intelligent young man, Darren, I expect better from you!'*

Comment quietly

Let me dissect this strategy a little. Walking slowly over to him, going down to his level and whispering the reprimand is calmly controlling and communicates respect. Whilst necessarily exercising your control over the child, it also shows that you are sensitive to his relationship with his friends. Addressing the behaviour first and concluding on the positive affirmation 'You are an intelligent young man' communicates the fact that it is not the child you dislike but just a certain aspect of his behaviour. This is important. Children will say that the teacher doesn't like them when, in fact, the teacher merely dislikes their behaviour at times.

If we address just the behaviour by using the technique described then the child is less likely to perceive the rebuke as being 'got at' and thus is less likely to initiate revenge strategies. And that is exactly what happens in the classroom. If, wherever possible, you tell a child off privately then that child is less likely to cause you further trouble.

The broken record technique

Repeat the comment

The Broken Record Technique is the calm repetition of a demand without allowing yourself to get drawn into argument. It has a rule of four for a troublesome boy and a rule of five for a troublesome girl! Let's pick on John this time!

> John, stop that.
> *It wasn't me, Miss.*
> John, stop that.
> *It was him, Miss.*
> John, stop that.
> *That's not fair.*
> John, stop that.

John has run out of things to say. You have used his limited verbal fluency against him! The challenging girl's response illuminates a major gender difference.

Cindy, stop that.
It wasn't me.
(The 'denial phase' is similar.)
Cindy, stop that.
You're always picking on me.
(She is much less likely than John to blame someone else. She now goes straight on to take it personally rather than applying the boy's exhortation to vague objective concepts such as fairness!)
Cindy stop that.
You did that to me yesterday!
(She reminds YOU of previous relationship violations!)
Cindy stop that.
I'll get you for this.
(Now comes the revenge!)
Cindy stop that.
(Silence now, save for a little under-the-breath mumbling to her friend!)

Girls invest a lot in their relationships. Boys' relationships tend to be more superficial and competitive. When two girls have a row with one another, the ramifications will last a long time. Boys fight at lunch-time and go home best of mates in the evening.

Tell a girl off and she'll sulk for ages. Tell a boy off and you can be friends with him a minute later. With a girl (or a spouse for that matter!) it is better for you to get her to tell herself off! It saves you the hassle. Girls and women are very self-critical …

Cindy, why have I come over to you?
Because I'm talking, Miss.
Thank you!

Discrepancy assertion

This is characterised by 'On the one hand ... on the other ...'. It is a useful way of pointing out inconsistencies in behaviour and challenging untruthful responses: '*On the one hand* you are telling me that you didn't do the graffiti, *on the other* there's paint on your hands!' I illustrate its use in the script that concludes the chapter.

Fogging

I especially recommend this technique!

What's wrong, Darren?
I'm bored!
<u>*Yes*</u>.
On with your work, please.

Fogging, characterised by the word 'yes', and followed by a simple instruction does not permit a child to manipulate the argument or dominate the exchange. Neither does it inform the child that he or she is wrong! After all, you do have to give children a few tasks that they will find boring, don't you?

Threaten before you punish

When you tell a child off, it is sometimes easier and less time consuming to make it simply an issue of authority rather than an attempt at behavioural modification! See below for an example.

The sequence to effective behaviour management is Predict–Prevent–Minimalise–Control. If you know that Darren and Wayne are bad news sitting together, don't let them sit together. Don't say to them, 'You can sit together this lesson if you promise to behave!' They won't and you know it. Say to them instead, 'You will be sitting separately this lesson. If you both behave well then you may sit together *next* lesson.'

When problems arise, seek firstly to minimalise them. That's where the Passing Technique, the Broken Record Technique, Discrepancy Assertion and Fogging come into their own. Control through sanction only as a last resort, use *Consequence Assertion* and make it an issue of authority, a personal one between you and the child: *'If you are not willing to co-operate with me, I will ...'*

Put these strategies together with the praise tenets in Chapter 8 and you have a script for excellent behaviour management in the classroom.

Darren goes to school

A playlet in one act with lots of disruptions (showing currently around the country with repeats daily!)

Stage directions and performance notes for the teacher are given in italics.

IT IS THE START OF THE LESSON. THE CLASSROOM IS NOISY. THE TEACHER MOVES CALMLY TO THE FRONT OF THE CLASS, ENGAGES THE CLASS BY MAKING EYE CONTACT WITH INDIVIDUAL CHILDREN AND SMILES.

Allow the class a few moments to settle themselves down. Don't say 'I'm waiting!' With difficult children, this statement is likely to be met by the response 'Who cares?'

THE TEACHER INDICATES WITH HER HAND TO BE QUIET AND VISUALLY PROMPTS THE ATTENTIVE PUPILS TO QUIETEN THOSE WHO ARE NOT.

Visual control devices are better than verbal ones.

TEACHER: Thank you, everyone.

---

continued

Initial instructions should anticipate compliance and praise it in advance. This is exactly what 'Thank you, everyone' does. It is the best way of starting a lesson. Most lessons start with the word 'Right!' It is much overused and consequently ineffective.

THE TEACHER IS NOT GETTING THE RESPONSE QUIETNESS SHE HAS ASKED FOR.

She should now consider whether or not she actually needs total silence before proceeding. Frequently, it is best to draw the pupils' attention in by a quick-fire dynamic start. She could use TALK WITH THE PERSON NEXT TO YOU, affording her an opportunity to have a quiet word with those not on task. But this time she does need everyone's undivided attention so she uses the Broken Record Technique to get it. Lower your voice to get quiet rather than raise it and slow down the repetition of the request.

TEACHER: Thank you, everyone. Thank you, everyone. Thank you!

DARREN ENTERS (LATE).

TEACHER: (QUIETLY) See me later, Darren.

She is using the Passing Technique.

DARREN: Why? What have I done?!

TEACHER: See me later, Darren. Thank you.

The Passing Technique is now supported by the Broken Record Technique. 'Thank you' said quietly, is a strong way of ending an argument with a boy before it starts! When you tell a child to stop doing something, use 'thank you' afterwards to stop the child arguing and to anticipate the expected change in behaviour.

DARREN SITS IN THE CORNER OF THE ROOM AND STARTS TO MISBEHAVE. THE TEACHER WALKS SLOWLY OVER TO HIM, TAKING THE ATTENTION OF THE REST OF THE CLASS WITH HER (THUS HELPING TO KEEP THEM QUIET) AND GOES DOWN TO HIS LEVEL.

TEACHER: Darren, stop mucking around, it's silly. You are really bright and you'll be good at this lesson. Get involved. Thank you.

She is using private rather than public reprimand and is clearly separating Darren from his behaviour.

continued

Now, if Darren's behaviour improves, catch him behaving better as soon as you can. Go over to him quietly and privately and thank him: 'Thank you, Darren, you are co-operating with me much better now. Well done!' It is remarkable how infrequently one sees teachers doing this. If we wish a child to continue behaving well, then we must show him or her that we have recognised the change in his or her behaviour and reward it.

THE TEACHER RETURNS TO THE FRONT OF THE CLASS AND DARREN THROWS A PAPER DART AT HER. THE TEACHER PICKS THE PAPER DART UP AND DROPS IT IN THE BIN.

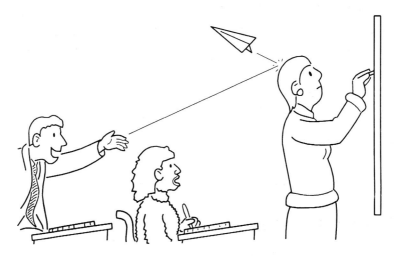

TEACHER: See me later, Darren!

Yes, the Passing Technique again! You can safely use it three times. Darren's behaviour was designed for confrontation. You should only confront a child's behaviour when you want to, not when the child wants you to. If the teacher were to confront this behaviour now, she would lay herself open to denial and Darren would get the confrontation he is looking for. Other boys may then adopt Darren's behaviour in a bid for attention.

Similarly, a teacher's early intervention can be counter-productive. It raises the stakes and entrenches positions and behaviours. Seek to minimalise before you control. Ignoring something can be a highly effective minimalisation strategy.

DARREN THROWS ANOTHER PAPER DART.

TEACHER: Pick it up please, Darren.

DARREN: It wasn't me!

TEACHER: Pick it up please, Darren.

The Broken Record Technique.

continued

Darren goes to school continued

DARREN: No, it wasn't me!

TEACHER: On the one hand, Darren, you are telling me it wasn't you, on the other hand, I saw you! Pick it up, please Darren. Thank you.

SHE TURNS HER BACK ON THE CHILD AND GIVES HIM A MOMENT TO COMPLY. HE DOESN'T.

TEACHER: (WITH A SMILE) See me later, Darren.

SHE PICKS UP THE PAPER DART AND DROPS IT IN THE BIN.

She has backed up the Broken Record Technique by Discrepancy Assertion. She issues the instruction again and stops the child arguing further by 'Thank you'.

(A similarly strong strategy for stopping argument is to say to the child, 'This is not a discussion, I'm telling you.' or 'If you think that I am being unfair then come and see me after the lesson.')

She now gives him an opportunity to comply without losing too much face by turning her back. He doesn't comply. No big deal! The smile and tone in her voice communicate that this is childish behaviour that she can easily deal with. She has used the Passing Technique, however, for the third and final time!

DARREN MISBEHAVES AGAIN! THE TEACHER WALKS OVER TO HIM.

TEACHER (QUIETLY):   Darren, this is a warning. If you are not willing to co-operate with me, I shall ask you to move to the front of the class. Thank you.

No vague statements about 'behaving better'. She has made it an issue of one-to-one authority. She has also warned first before punishing. It is now all very clear to the child where continued poor behaviour will lead. When you threaten a child with a sanction then never go back on your word. Darren must now be punished if he continues with his disruptive behaviour.

AFTER A FEW MOMENTS, DARREN MISBEHAVES AGAIN. THE TEACHER CARRIES A CHAIR OVER TO DARREN, PLACES IT IN FRONT OF HIM AND, WITHOUT SAYING A WORD, INDICATES FOR HIM TO TAKE THE CHAIR TO THE FRONT OF THE CLASS. HE REFUSES. SHE IGNORES THE REFUSAL, RETURNS TO THE FRONT OF THE CLASS BUT LEAVES THE CHAIR IN FRONT OF DARREN!

continued

Get real! The last thing you want is Darren at the front of the class. You want him to sulk quietly so you, in turn, can have a quiet word with him. If this is indeed what you want, then the strategy of taking the chair over to him is likely to produce the desired effect. Done calmly and assertively without saying anything, far from being a weak response, it is a technique that has a powerful and controlling effect on the rest of the class. You are not one to be easily rattled.

DARREN CONTINUES TO BE DISRUPTIVE. THE TEACHER GOES OVER TO HIM.

TEACHER: Darren, I asked you to move to the front of the class and you refused. If you do not now move to the front of the class, you will be in detention.

Notice the opt-out clause. He can take up the original sanction. Or he decides to increase the penalty for his poor behaviour. Either way he has lost! The teacher has stayed quietly in control and her calm assertive manner is most likely to have calmed Darren's behaviour.

The extended and sequential nature of this process, although taking up classroom time initially, pays dividends in the longer term. Communicate your expectations and your classroom rules and, above all else, be calm and consistent. Remember, after all is said and done, that you are an adult and they are children. You are the responsible one. Responsible meaning 'the ability to choose a response'. I hope the above gives you a few more responses to choose from.

Empowerment

If you find classroom control easy and have developed a good relationship with your class, then you now have an opportunity to do something special. You have the opportunity to teach the children an important life skill. Boys tend to be aggressive rather than assertive. Girls tend to be passive rather than assertive. You can use classroom interactions to train all pupils in how to be assertive.

Teach assertion

First, define your expectations of behaviour in the classroom and communicate your classroom rules clearly and explicitly. Discuss the reasons behind these rules and expectations.

Now ask the class to brainstorm and define their expectations of *each other's* behaviour. From these, produce a few simple guidelines to good behaviour in your classroom, for example:

- We don't laugh at other people's ideas.
- We don't interrupt one another.
- We don't distract one another from our learning.
- We don't bully one another.

Next, discuss with the class what constitutes assertive rather than aggressive behaviour and translate the rules that they have developed into assertive responses, thus:

- Don't laugh at me, please.
- Please let me finish what I am saying.
- Would you be quiet, please? I am working.
- Don't do that.

Give the class practice in saying these responses, calmly and quietly to one another in pairs.

Finally, inform the class that you will be enforcing your classroom rules calmly and assertively and you will be requiring them to do the same. If a child is laughed at then you are going to ask that child to stand up for themselves by saying 'Don't laugh at me, please'. If someone is being noisy, you will ask a pupil nearby to say 'Would you be quiet, please?' and so on.

You now have a powerful tool not only to teach young people how to be assertive but also for helping them to manage their own behaviour in the classroom. Difficult Darren is likely to be the first child to start doing it. He will do it in a testing and aggressive manner at first by yelling, 'Shut up!' Meet this by 'OK, Darren, now say it again, only assertively this time!' Next time you need the class to be silent, ask Darren to get everyone quiet for you!

Public reprimand

I previously discussed the need for the quiet word rather than the public rebuke. There is an important time, however, when the public reprimand is called for. In the classroom, we manage two things. We manage our relationship with the class and individuals within that class, but we also need to manage the pupil–pupil relationships as well. Boys, with their poorer social skills, are more likely to need the latter than girls. A child needs to feel safe and secure if he or she is to flourish. Bullying, in any form, jeopardises the safety of the learning environment. It is the foremost concern of most children in school. A pupil-to-pupil violation of any kind should always be dealt with publicly in front of the whole class.

Given the assertiveness training above, we might now deal with such incidents in a positive and empowering way.

Wherever the genders or the races meet, sexual or racial harassment is a fact of life. Such incidents may be perceived as additional types of bullying. Boys bully other boys and girls bully other girls. Yet more boys will attempt to put down or bully girls than vice versa. Thus, the average girl has additional types of bullying to deal with, the many forms of sexual harassment. Similarly the black or Asian child is likely to suffer an additional detriment, that is, the many forms of racial harassment. Dealing with such incidents effectively is fundamental to good Equal Opportunities practice. For the more 'minor' sexist or racist incidents in the classroom, stop the lesson and handle the incident in this way ...

'John, stop that. It's sexual harassment/it's bullying/it's racist.
Cindy/Balbir, if he does that again you should tell him to stop it.
If he doesn't stop it, then you should tell me.
John, you are an intelligent young man, I expect better of you.
If I don't treat you with the respect you deserve then tell me.
Cindy/Balbir, have I done enough about that for the moment?
OK, let's spend a moment to look at why this issue
is so important to us all ...' DEBRIEF WITH THE CLASS.

In the context of a book about improving boys' performance, it is important to point out that racism is likely to have a significant effect upon especially (although, of course, not exclusively) the black or Asian boys' achievement. Cultural exclusion, for example, may further compound gender exclusion.

Antiracist policy and practice guidelines

- Staff, pupils and parents should understand the significant differences in racist and sexist behaviour to other forms of bullying / anti-social behaviour.

- All teachers should make a special point of *publicly* challenging racist sentiments, attitudes, expressions and behaviour. The challenges should be positive – separating the person from his or her mistake – and be debriefed with the whole class.

- Incidents of more serious racial insult or attack should be dealt with in a consistent and firm way by someone of high status within the organisation. These incidents should be monitored.

- Teachers should facilitate mixed-race group work.

- Assemblies should refer to the effect of racism and prejudice and communicate the school's policy and practice.

- Displays, textbooks and school publications should be sensitive to multiracial considerations.

- Periodically, the school should mount special Equal Opportunities events.

- Departments within the school should utilise multicultural potentials within their subject areas.

An example of a whole-school, multicultural approach

ENGLISH uses texts throughout the curriculum from which the department selects areas where discussion on antiracism and multicultural themes may be facilitated by the class teacher.

RE/HUMANITIES have modules on Prejudice in Year 7 (S1) and 'Racism in England' in Year 10 (S4).

HISTORY includes in its syllabus the Colonialisation of South Africa and the development of the Islamic Nations.

GEOGRAPHY uses the Rain Forest Child pack in Year 9 (S3).

SCIENCE explores the contributions of black and Asian scientists.

BUSINESS STUDIES exploits the multicultural elements in the Economic and Industrial Understanding themes of the National Curriculum.

TECHNOLOGY leads a cross-curricular technology theme in Year 9 (S3): 'Celebrations throughout the world'.

PE exploits the potential of African rhythms and Asian Bhangra in Year 10 (S4) dance and runs a 'Children's games around the world' project in Year 7 (S1).

MODERN LANGUAGES runs Language Awareness courses for all pupils and includes Non-European languages and references.

MATHS utilises the potential of Non-European contributions to mathematical understanding (e.g. the Vedic Square).

DRAMA mounts a presentation by GCSE pupils for school assemblies on an Equal Opportunities theme and explores racism, sexism and prejudice within its curriculum.

Attitudes and success

Our attitudes are highly significant to our sense of self. By challenging negative attitudes such as racism or sexism, we help children to form a connection between their own identity and their attitudes to others. Successful pupils, in common with successful people, have five core strengths:

1. High self-esteem/ confidence level

Racist attitudes frequently indicate a person of low self-esteem whose accumulated experience of failure may lead them to victimisation and a need of scapegoats as defence mechanisms for their own feelings of inadequacy. Tolerance and understanding are virtues indicative of successful and self-confident people with positive attitudes to themselves.

Successful challenges to racism may be made on this level: *'You are an intelligent young man/woman ... you don't need to put other people down in this way!'* or *'You're a kind person and that's a very good quality. I'm surprised that you're expressing such intolerant views.'*

2. Good reflective thinkers

Racist attitudes indicate someone who is more likely to accept 'received ideas' rather than think things through for him or herself.

Successful challenges to racism may be made on this level: *'I am surprised at you thinking this way. You're good at making up your own mind. It seems as though you are repeating other people's views without thinking them through yourself.'* Or with challenges than demand reflective analysis, such as *'If black people take our jobs, why are there proportionately more black people unemployed than white people?'* or *'What do you mean by OUR jobs?'*

3. Risk-takers

Risk-taking requires a high confidence level and the ability to cope positively with failure. It is high-order ASSERTIVE behaviour. Racist behaviour is AGGRESSIVE which, in itself, is often a response to feeling threatened or inadequate. It is frequently indicative of someone who struggles to gain control of forces beyond them and who is *risk-averse*.

Successful challenges to racism may be made on this level: *'You are someone who is capable of risking your own views, rather than repeating those of others!'* or *'You are someone who is capable of expressing your own views rather than needing to follow the crowd and complying with the views of those around you!'*

4. Good at working with others

Less secure people are comfortable only with working with those they know. Insecure people may need the protection of 'tribal behaviour' and strong enforcement of group identity to find value for themselves.

Successful challenges to racism may be made on this level: *'To be successful, you need to be able to work well with lots of different people. You're confident enough to do this, I'm sure!'*

5. Non-stereotypical

Racist attitudes are based on received ideas and ignorance. Respect for others is indicative of self-respect and autonomous thinking, rather than stereotypical attitudes. Schools are organisations founded on knowledge, understanding, mutual respect and tolerance.

Challenge stereotypical behaviour: *'That's rather stereotypical, isn't it? I'm surprised at you, Darren!'* And, of course, explain what you mean.

THE THREE Rs in the chapter title are 'RESPECT, RESPECT, RESPECT!' Let me end these two chapters on behaviour management with some school rules.

School rules *for teachers*

1. I must behave in a respectful way to my class at all times. For only by showing respect will I ever gain respect.

2. I must accept responsibility. If pupils misbehave, it is MY fault. I have not stretched and challenged them enough. I have not given them appropriate tasks. I have not given them enough praise. I have not taught them how to behave well. I am the adult. I should be able to choose my response. I should not blame children for my own inadequacies.

3. I must bring my equipment with me to lessons: high expectations, understanding, care and integrity.

4. No chewing. Do I like it when others chew me?

5. I must always wear my school uniform: do as I do rather than do what I say.

6. I must remember that school rules are designed first and foremost as opportunities for praise and reward and not as licence for punishment. I should only punish a child when I am in no way to blame.

7. I must understand that certain rights bear no responsibilities. All children in my care have an inalienable right to their education, their dignity and their self-esteem.

For good reasons, each of the above rules may be broken except this one:
THE CHILD COMES FIRST.

Chapter
10 *Whole-school developments*

To effect change, clear understandings are required. To begin with, one needs to appreciate the practical differences between the following:

VISION AND MISSION
LEADERSHIP AND MANAGEMENT
IMPORTANT AND URGENT

Vision and mission

The vision is how you wish things to be in the future. The clearer the vision is, the more likely you are to achieve it. The mission is how exactly you are going to achieve the vision. A mission statement begins with the word 'by'.

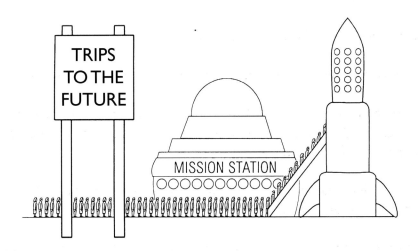

Leadership and management

Leaders lead the vision. Managers manage the mission (see above!).

Important and urgent

The important might not actually have to be done and, for that reason, gets all too often swamped by the urgent. Probably everything that's lasting in its importance is important *but* not urgent. It is important to eat your five portions of fruit and vegetables a day but it isn't urgent so the chocolate bar seduces your attention from the fruit bowl. Who, at retirement, looks back and thinks 'I wish I had worked more'? Commonly, the thought is 'I wish I had spent more time with my children while they were growing up!' Spending time with your family is important but not urgent. Neglect the important but not urgent things in life and you live to regret them! All the ideas in this book are of the important but not urgent type. It probably isn't urgent to develop pupil group work skills. They'll get by without them. But what kind of a future world are we creating for our children where Darren and Cindy don't have the skills to get on with one another? Do the urgent, sure, but concentrate most of your energies on the important. Here are some important strategies to affect whole-school development.

Head of department support time

Observing team members

A head of department commonly has five non-contact periods a week. The strategy of Support Time is to ensure that one of these periods is spent in the classroom observing and working with a department team member. This support period should be used to develop a specific teaching strategy.

If, for the important reasons explained in Chapter 4, you wish to develop pupil interactions in the classroom through a more structured approach to pair and group work then an HoD now has important but not urgent time set aside to facilitate the development. They could, for example, plan and teach a lesson through group work *together* to explore the new approach. Or the HoD might take the lesson and demonstrate a way of doing it for her colleague. The planning and delivery of Head of Department Support Time can in itself facilitate the desired development, that is, if the objectives of the observation are defined clearly and simply enough. For example, an HoD tells a team member that, in order to monitor the department's Action Plan to improve proximal learning, she will be observing a lesson next week. Perhaps the colleague hasn't, until now, developed a teaching style to include group work. He or she is now busy planning a first group work lesson and the children (who come first!) are now getting a little more access to learning.

The proactive structuring of Head of Department Support Time by, for example, including it in the school timetable and ensuring that cover is avoided at that time will mean that an HoD with a five-strong team might be in with each teacher once every five weeks. Tailor the observation simply and precisely to your mission statement and your children now get 40 good quality pair and group work lessons a year where previously they had none!

Head of year support time

Observing pupils

Structure important but not urgent time in a similar way for a head of year and they have time now to extract their list of Darrens and Matthews from the database and see these children individually or in groups to target improvements through the merit system. They also have time to be in subject lessons with the children in their year group (an important and generally underused approach in schools' pastoral processes). They might help the subject teacher during the lesson.

Hey, what's this the head of year discovers during his visit? His visit coincides with HoD Support Time. The department head and the class teacher are working together to improve group work. What an opportunity! He is going to award extra merit points during the lesson to pupils who co-operate well with others.

Of course, this was planned in advance. SMT know that to develop Collective Management and a Shared Vision the best way is to dovetail developmental initiatives.

Senior management support time

Cascading strategies

Important time here is planned *in advance* for a senior manager to work with a middle manager to discuss how a specific initiative will be both led and managed by that middle manager.

Just as the head of department and head of year have time set aside for their central pupil and staff management functions, so, too, should the senior manager spend time supporting his or her charges and observe them at work in the classroom. For example, the development initiative is to use GOING FOR FIVE to develop the boys' planning skills. The senior manager discusses how this might be done in science with the head of department. 'When I come in to observe your lesson next week, can you focus on GOING FOR FIVE and then we can discuss how we can develop it with the rest of your team?' The head of department is helped to clarify the strategy and plan how it may be cascaded. That HoD has her own support time in place to do it.

Headteacher support time

Observing in the classroom

OK, you are an incredibly busy person with lots of urgent things on your desk! It is important for you, Head, to get into the classroom and observe – in free market terms, to access your client base and gauge consumer reaction! In my experience, Headteachers do not find enough time to spend in the classroom: time to lead through example; time to check up that developments are actually taking place. How else do you do it but by being there yourself at the point of delivery, at the chalk-face?

The important issue

Schools are engaging in an increasing level of observation. The problem is likely to be that it isn't being done consistently enough or with enough precision. Observers wander around the classroom with enormous check-lists. I'll give you one myself at the end of this chapter (p.94)! What is required are observers who are looking for the core and important elements in learning and for these observers to be able to make simple suggestions on how things might be improved. These are given on the following pages.

Headteacher	Monitor especially the *praise levels* you observe in the classroom. Ensure they stay well above 3:1.
	Request that departments present you personally with a breakdown of the merit awards they give and the sanctions they enforce. It is common for high achieving departments to be high on the list of merits and low on the list of sanctions. The underperforming departments are likely to be bottom of the ranking with more sanctions given than rewards. The remedy is sweet and simple. Tell the underperforming departments to give more merits and check that they do.
Deputies	Concentrate your observational energies into looking for *step-by-step approaches* to teaching. The excellent lesson will have between three and five steps (revise Chapter 5!).
Head of department	Look for how *interactive* the teaching is. Observe how the teacher activates proximal as well as individual learning.
	Ensure that there is enough variety and that the children are spending enough time in reading and not too much time in writing. Think ratios (see Chapters 6 and 7).
Class teacher	Spend enough time overtly teaching the children *how* to do things (Chapter 7) and do it in a varied, exciting and challenging way (the rest of the book!).
Form tutor	Ensure that each of your children spends some time with you on a *one-to-one* basis. You could arrange this during assemblies, for example.
	Show interest in their work and how they feel they are getting along. Monitor academic progress and set realistic and attainable targets with them. But most of all, find time to do the important and simple human thing of getting to know them as individual people.
Head of year	Don't spend too much of your time doing what others believe to be urgent. You should not spend your time telling children off and dealing with your colleagues' problems for them.
	You are there for the important job of *pupil counselling, motivation* and *support*. Monitor effort and behaviour and target-set with children to improve their performance.
Parents	Get them involved. Raise *awareness* with the parents on the issues underlying boys' attainment.
	Make suggestions, even run workshops, on how they can support their child's learning in the home (see the section on homework in Chapter 8).

Pupils

Raise *awareness* and convey this message! Successful people are not stereotypical.

Successful men are natural risk-takers and doers but they are *also* good thinkers and good planners.

Successful women, although naturally good at planning and detail, are *also* good risk-takers.

Successful pupils have the skills of both the genders. Boys and girls should have their fun but should seize their opportunities as well.

A Strategy check-list for improving the performance of boys is given on p.94.

Improving boys' performance: Strategy check-list

Communicate challenge
Define purpose
Prescribe time limits
Go for quality
Use a variety of approaches
Use quizzes
Assess gains in learning

GO FOR FIVE and use five steps
Use templates

Apply a pluralistic approach to pupil groupings
Develop structured proximal learning
Teach group work skills
Develop communication skills
Structure on-task talk

Teach step by step
Teach **Descriptive–Reflective–Speculative**

Write for purpose
Teach linking words
Teach pupils how to write using D–R–S

Read to reinforce knowledge
Read to interact through speculation
Read to record information
Read to be critical
Read to teach others
Use paired reading

Teach **how** before why
Think **ratios**

Praise
Monitor
Target praise

Non-confrontational assertion
The passing technique
Private rather than public reprimand
Broken record
Discrepancy assertion
Fogging
Respect, respect, respect

Manage change
Head of department support time
Head of year support time
Headteacher and SMT support time

Vision
Concentrate on the important

Postscript: The future

We need to teach children rather than subjects. For too long now, we have concentrated our educational energies on what to teach children rather than how children learn. Rather than a content-driven National Curriculum, we need a competency-driven approach. Children need to read and write but they also need to work well with others. If you need information and fact, then turn on your computer. If you want to learn to think, then call on a teacher. Give me wisdom rather than knowledge.

Our pedagogy should focus on how we teach children, not on what we teach them. Our curriculum should be founded on respect for its recipients – a respect that values childhood as a valid state in itself and not merely as a preparation for adulthood.

Education should not be elitist, socially divisive, or exclusive. We should not permit ill-defined concepts such as 'ability' to prescribe academic failure and low self-esteem to a large group of mostly boys through the misguided practice of streaming and setting. Every child is a mixed-ability child. Every child needs a good mixed-ability classroom.

The provision of real equality of opportunity will only happen when we stop treating everyone the same. Boys and girls are clearly not the same.

Understandably, in the past, we were reticent in speaking about differences because difference can so readily imply value judgements. Alas, in a society still afflicted by sexism and racism, caution is still needed. The battle for female equality is being won but it isn't won yet. To say that women and men are likely to differ in some important aspects is not to say that one is better than the other or that one is necessarily better than the other in any of their endeavours. What we value most in ourselves is not our similarities but our own unique differences. Valuing difference leads us to understanding and to the greatest gift that educators might bestow upon future generations: tolerance.

Further reading

Anne and Bill Moir, *Why Men Don't Iron: The Real Science of Gender Studies* (Channel Four Books, 1999)
ISBN 0–00–257035–1

Jon Pickering, *Raising Boys' Achievement* (Network Press, 1997)
ISBN 1–85539–040–X

SHA, *Can Boys Do Better?* (April 1997)
ISBN 0–909916 41 0

Contact

Geoff Hannan and Angela Hannan
Training and Consultancy International
Bank Cottage
Bourton Rd
Much Wenlock
Shropshire TF13 6AJ
Phone (44) 0 1952 727332